Edna Hobbs has been teaching English since 1984. In the 1990s she took a second degree through the Open University, studying Shakespeare's plays exclusively in one module. *Much* Ado is one of her favourite plays. At present she teaches English at a secondary school in Dorset, also contributi teaching websites and magazines as the opportunity arises.

I think Shakespeare knew a thing or two about love; especially, he knew th word- not just a noun, or name. I dedicate this resource to my family, who powering my life. And I dedicate it to you, studying for exams – may you or Shakespeare as sheer entertainment and profound wisdom at the same tim

Mr Bruff would like to thank:

- Sam Perkins, who designed the front cover of this eBook.
- Sunny Ratilal, who designed the original front cover which was adapted for this edition.

Contents

Act 1 Scene 1

ORIGINAL TEXT	MODERN TRANSLATION
Before LEONATO'S house.	**In front of LEONATO'S house**
Enter LEONATO, HERO, and BEATRICE, with a MESSENGER	*Enter LEONATO, HERO, his daughter, and BEATRICE, his niece, with a MESSENGER*
LEONATO I learn in this letter that Don Pedro of Aragon comes this night to Messina.	**LEONATO** *(reading a letter)* This letter says Don Pedro of Aragon is coming to Messina tonight.
MESSENGER He is very near by this: he was not three leagues off when I left him.	**MESSENGER** He is very near here: he was about nine miles away when I left him.
LEONATO How many gentlemen have you lost in this action?	**LEONATO** How many noblemen died in the battle?
MESSENGER But few of any sort, and none of name.	**MESSENGER** Very few, and no one important.
LEONATO A victory is twice itself when the achiever brings home full numbers. I find here that Don Pedro hath bestowed much honour on a young Florentine called Claudio.	**LEONATO** It's a double victory when you both win the battle and also bring your soldiers home safely. .. I read in my letter that Don Pedro has given honours to a young man from Florence called Claudio.
MESSENGER Much deserved on his part and equally remembered by Don Pedro: he hath borne himself beyond the promise of his age, doing, in the figure of a lamb, the feats of a lion: he hath indeed better bettered expectation than you must expect of me to tell you how.	**MESSENGER** Claudio really deserved it and Don Pedro has suitably rewarded him: Claudio has been braver than you'd expect from someone of his age, like a lamb fighting with a lion's courage: he's done so well that I can't to tell you of all the details now.
LEONATO He hath an uncle here in Messina will be very much glad of it.	**LEONATO** He has an uncle here in Messina who will be very proud and delighted to hear this news.
MESSENGER I have already delivered him letters, and there appears much joy in him; even so much that joy could not show itself modest enough without a badge of bitterness.	**MESSENGER** I have already delivered some letters to him, and he was so overjoyed he actually looked as though he was in pain.
LEONATO Did he break out into tears?	**LEONATO** Did he burst into tears?
MESSENGER In great measure.	**MESSENGER** Yes, he cried a lot.

LEONATO A kind overflow of kindness: there are no faces truer than those that are so washed. How much better is it to weep at joy than to joy at weeping!	**LEONATO** He was literally overflowing with emotion: his tears show how much it meant to him. It's far better to cry with joy than to enjoy crying!
BEATRICE I pray you, is Signor Mountanto returned from the wars or no?	**BEATRICE** Please tell me, has Sir Mountanto (Mr 'Social Climber') returned from the battle or not?
MESSENGER I know none of that name, lady: there was none such in the army of any sort.	**MESSENGER** I don't know of anyone with that name, lady: there was no Sir Mountanto in our army.
LEONATO What is he that you ask for, niece?	**LEONATO** Who are you talking about, niece?
HERO My cousin means Signor Benedick of Padua.	**HERO** My cousin means Sir Benedick of Padua.
MESSENGER O, he's returned; and as pleasant as ever he was.	**MESSENGER** O, yes, Benedick has returned; and is as nice as always.
BEATRICE He set up his bills here in Messina and challenged Cupid at the flight; and my uncle's fool, reading the challenge, subscribed for Cupid, and challenged him at the bird-bolt. I pray you, how many hath he killed and eaten in these wars? But how many hath he killed? for indeed I promised to eat all of his killing.	**BEATRICE** Benedick challenged Cupid to an archery contest here in Messina, publicly boasting he could make more women fall in love with him than Cupid's arrows could hit; and my uncle's jester, reading the challenge, accepted on Cupid's behalf but used blunt arrows normally used for shooting birds at close range. Tell me, how many men has Benedick killed and eaten in these wars? Or more importantly, how many has he killed? Because I actually promised to eat anyone he killed.
LEONATO Faith, niece, you tax Signor Benedick too much; but he'll be meet with you, I doubt it not.	**LEONATO** Good grief, Beatrice! You insult Sir Benedick too much; but I'm sure he'll get even.
MESSENGER He hath done good service, lady, in these wars.	**MESSENGER** He has proved a good soldier, lady, in these wars.
BEATRICE You had musty victual, and he hath holp to eat it: he is a very valiant trencherman; he hath an excellent stomach.	**BEATRICE** You had rotten food, and he helped you to eat it: he is a very brave eater; he has an excellent stomach.
MESSENGER And a good soldier too, lady.	**MESSENGER** He is a good soldier too, lady.
BEATRICE And a good soldier to a lady: but what is he to a lord?	**BEATRICE** And a good soldier to a lady: but what is he to a lord?
MESSENGER A lord to a lord, a man to a man; stuffed with all honourable virtues.	**MESSENGER** A lord to a lord, a man to a man; he is stuffed full of honourable virtues.

BEATRICE It is so, indeed; he is no less than a stuffed man: but for the stuffing,--well, we are all mortal.	**BEATRICE** Absolutely; he is stuffed, like a dummy: but as for the stuffing,--well, no body is perfect.
LEONATO You must not, sir, mistake my niece. There is a kind of merry war betwixt Signor Benedick and her: they never meet but there's a skirmish of wit between them.	**LEONATO** Please don't misunderstand my niece. There is a kind of enjoyable banter between Benedick and her: whenever they meet they try to outwit each other.
BEATRICE Alas! he gets nothing by that. In our last conflict four of his five wits went halting off, and now is the whole man governed with one: so that if he have wit enough to keep himself warm, let him bear it for a difference between himself and his horse; for it is all the wealth that he hath left, to be known a reasonable creature. Who is his companion now? He hath every month a new sworn brother.	**BEATRICE** Poor dear! He never wins. In our last clash he was so confused he wasn't much cleverer than his horse; all he has in his favour is that people think he's reasonable. Who is his best friend now? Every month he has a new blood brother.
MESSENGER Is't possible?	**MESSENGER** Is that possible?
BEATRICE Very easily possible: he wears his faith but as the fashion of his hat; it ever changes with the next block.	**BEATRICE** Very easily possible: his loyalty changes as easily and as often as the style of his hat.
MESSENGER I see, lady, the gentleman is not in your books.	**MESSENGER** I see, lady, you don't like him: he's obviously not in your good books.
BEATRICE No; an he were, I would burn my study. But, I pray you, who is his companion? Is there no young squarer now that will make a voyage with him to the devil?	**BEATRICE** No; and if he were, I'd burn my library. But tell me, who is his new best friend? Is there no young warrior who'll travel with him to hell and back?
MESSENGER He is most in the company of the right noble Claudio.	**MESSENGER** He mostly hangs around the honourable nobleman Claudio.
BEATRICE O Lord, he will hang upon him like a disease: he is sooner caught than the pestilence, and the taker runs presently mad. God help the noble Claudio! if he have caught the Benedick, it will cost him a thousand pound ere a' be cured.	**BEATRICE** O Lord, Benedick will stick to him like a disease: he is an infection more easily caught than the plague, driving those he plagues mad. God help the noble Claudio! If he has caught 'the Benedick', he'll be taking on an expensive friend.
MESSENGER I will hold friends with you, lady.	**MESSENGER** I'll stay friends with you, lady.
BEATRICE Do, good friend.	**BEATRICE** Please do, good friend.

LEONATO You will never run mad, niece.	**LEONATO** You'll never fall madly in love, niece.
BEATRICE No, not till a hot January.	**BEATRICE** No, not until January is a hot month.
MESSENGER Don Pedro is approached.	**MESSENGER** Don Pedro is arriving.
Enter DON PEDRO, DON JOHN, CLAUDIO, BENEDICK, and BALTHASAR	*Enter DON PEDRO, DON JOHN, CLAUDIO, BENEDICK, and BALTHASAR*
DON PEDRO Good Signor Leonato, you are come to meet your trouble: the fashion of the world is to avoid cost, and you encounter it.	**DON PEDRO** Good Sir Leonato, most people avoid trouble, yet you welcome us: most people avoid cost, yet you come to meet me and my expensive army.
LEONATO Never came trouble to my house in the likeness of your grace: for trouble being gone, comfort should remain; but when you depart from me, sorrow abides and happiness takes his leave.	**LEONATO** You are no trouble, your Grace: when trouble goes away, it's a relief; but when you leave me, happiness goes with you and sorrow remains.
DON PEDRO You embrace your charge too willingly. I think this is your daughter.	**DON PEDRO** You accept the role of host too willingly. (turning to HERO) I think this is your daughter.
LEONATO Her mother hath many times told me so.	**LEONATO** Her mother has often told me so.
BENEDICK Were you in doubt, sir, that you asked her?	**BENEDICK** Did you doubt it, sir- is that why you asked her?
LEONATO Signor Benedick, no; for then were you a child.	**LEONATO** No Sir Benedick , because you were only a child at the time, too young to seduce my wife.
DON PEDRO You have it full, Benedick: we may guess by this what you are, being a man. Truly, the lady fathers herself. Be happy, lady; for you are like an honourable father.	**DON PEDRO** Ha, burn Benedick! Leonarto knows your reputation! Truly, the lady looks like her father. Be happy, lady; for you resemble an honourable man.
BENEDICK If Signor Leonato be her father, she would not have his head on her shoulders for all Messina, as like him as she is.	**BENEDICK** Well, even if Sir Leonato is her father, she wouldn't want to have his head on her shoulders for all Messina, even if she is like him.
BEATRICE I wonder that you will still be talking, Signor Benedick: nobody marks you.	**BEATRICE** I 'm surprised you're still talking, Sir Benedick: nobody takes any notice of you.
BENEDICK What, my dear Lady Disdain! are you yet living?	**BENEDICK** What, my dear Lady Disdain! Are you still alive?

BEATRICE Is it possible disdain should die while she hath such meet food to feed it as Signor Benedick? Courtesy itself must convert to disdain, if you come in her presence.	**BEATRICE** How could disdain die while she has you to feed on? Courtesy itself must become disdain, if you come into her presence.
BENEDICK Then is courtesy a turncoat. But it is certain I am loved of all ladies, only you excepted: and I would I could find in my heart that I had not a hard heart; for, truly, I love none.	**BENEDICK** Then is courtesy a traitor. All ladies love me except for you: what a shame I'm so hard-hearted I love no one.
BEATRICE A dear happiness to women: they would else have been troubled with a pernicious suitor. I thank God and my cold blood, I am of your humour for that: I had rather hear my dog bark at a crow than a man swear he loves me.	**BEATRICE** How lucky for women: now at least they won't be bothered by a spiteful suitor. Thankfully I'm as cold-blooded as you are: I would rather hear my dog bark at a crow than a man say he loves me.
BENEDICK God keep your ladyship still in that mind! so some gentleman or other shall 'scape a predestinate scratched face.	**BENEDICK** I hope to God you won't change your mind! Otherwise some gentleman or other will end up with a scratched face.
BEATRICE Scratching could not make it worse, an 'twere such a face as yours were.	**BEATRICE** Scratching could not make it worse, if he looked like you.
BENEDICK Well, you are a rare parrot-teacher.	**BENEDICK** Well, you are parroting everything I say!
BEATRICE A bird of my tongue is better than a beast of yours.	**BEATRICE** Well a squawking bird is better than being a beast.
BENEDICK I would my horse had the speed of your tongue, and so good a continuer. But keep your way, i' God's name; I have done.	**BENEDICK** I wish my horse was as fast and tireless as your tongue. But that's enough; I've finished.
BEATRICE You always end with a jade's trick: I know you of old.	**BEATRICE** You always end the argument so that you can have the last word: I know you well.
DON PEDRO That is the sum of all, Leonato. Signor Claudio and Signor Benedick, my dear friend Leonato hath invited you all. I tell him we shall stay here at the least a month; and he heartily prays some occasion may detain us longer. I dare swear he is no hypocrite, but prays from his heart.	**DON PEDRO** (who has been chatting quietly to Leonarto) That is all the news, Leonato. Sir Claudio and Sir Benedick, my dear friend Leonato has invited you all to stay here. I've told him we'll stay here at least a month, but he says he hopes we stay longer. I'm sure he means it too, its not just good manners.
LEONATO If you swear, my lord, you shall not be forsworn. *To DON JOHN*	**LEONATO** I am serious, my lord *To DON JOHN*

Let me bid you welcome, my lord: being reconciled to the prince your brother, I owe you all duty.	Welcome, my lord: now that you're at peace with the prince your brother, I owe you the same loyalty as I owe Don Pedro.
DON JOHN I thank you: I am not of many words, but I thank you.	**DON JOHN** I thank you: I don't say much, but I thank you.
LEONATO Please it your grace lead on?	**LEONATO** Would you please lead us all inside your grace?
DON PEDRO Your hand, Leonato; we will go together.	**DON PEDRO** Give me your hand, Leonato; we will go together.
Exeunt all except BENEDICK and CLAUDIO	*Exit all except BENEDICK and CLAUDIO*
CLAUDIO Benedick, didst thou note the daughter of Signor Leonato?	**CLAUDIO** Benedick, did you notice Sir Leonato's daughter?
BENEDICK I noted her not; but I looked on her.	**BENEDICK** I saw her; but I didn't notice her.
CLAUDIO Is she not a modest young lady?	**CLAUDIO** Isn't she the ideal young lady?
BENEDICK Do you question me, as an honest man should do, for my simple true judgment; or would you have me speak after my custom, as being a professed tyrant to their sex?	**BENEDICK** Do you want my true opinion; or do you want one of my speciality full-on criticisms of her as another woman to mock? I'm known as a woman-hater.
CLAUDIO No; I pray thee speak in sober judgment.	**CLAUDIO** No; please speak truthfully.
BENEDICK Why, i' faith, methinks she's too low for a high praise, too brown for a fair praise and too little for a great praise: only this commendation I can afford her, that were she other than she is, she were unhandsome; and being no other but as she is, I do not like her.	**BENEDICK** Well, I think she's too short for a high praise, too dark to be praised fairly and too small for a great praise: I can only say, if she wasn't so well connected and wealthy she'd be ugly; and even being who she is, I do not like her.
CLAUDIO Thou thinkest I am in sport: I pray thee tell me truly how thou likest her.	**CLAUDIO** You think I'm joking: please tell me honestly what you think of her.
BENEDICK Would you buy her, that you inquire after her?	**BENEDICK** Are you asking because you want to buy her?
CLAUDIO Can the world buy such a jewel?	**CLAUDIO** Is it possible to buy such a treasure?
BENEDICK Yea, and a case to put it into. But speak you this with a sad brow? or do you play the flouting Jack, to tell us Cupid is a good hare-finder and Vulcan a	**BENEDICK** Yes, and a case to put it into. But are you serious? or are you just messing about, having a laugh? Come

rare carpenter? Come, in what key shall a man take you, to go in the song?	on, if you want me to sing along with you, I need to know what key you're singing in.
CLAUDIO In mine eye she is the sweetest lady that ever I looked on.	**CLAUDIO** To my eye she is the sweetest lady that I ever saw.
BENEDICK I can see yet without spectacles and I see no such matter: there's her cousin, an she were not possessed with a fury, exceeds her as much in beauty as the first of May doth the last of December. But I hope you have no intent to turn husband, have you?	**BENEDICK** I can see without spectacles and I don't see it: her cousin, on the other hand – if she wasn't so bad-tempered- is so much more beautiful than Hero it's like comparing the first of May with the last of December. But I hope you're not thinking of marriage, are you?
CLAUDIO I would scarce trust myself, though I had sworn the contrary, if Hero would be my wife.	**CLAUDIO** Even if I had sworn never to marry, I would not trust myself to keep that promise if Hero agreed to be my wife.
BENEDICK Is't come to this? In faith, hath not the world one man but he will wear his cap with suspicion? Shall I never see a bachelor of three-score again? Go to, i' faith; an thou wilt needs thrust thy neck into a yoke, wear the print of it and sigh away Sundays. Look Don Pedro is returned to seek you.	**BENEDICK** Has it come to this? Is there no man left who can avoid marriage and the risk of being cheated on? Will I never see a sixty year old bachelor again? Go ahead and you'll be thrusting your neck into a yoke, like an ox. The burden of it will scar you and even Sundays won't be free. Look Don Pedro has come looking for you.
Re-enter DON PEDRO	*Re-enter DON PEDRO*
DON PEDRO What secret hath held you here, that you followed not to Leonato's?	**DON PEDRO** What secrets have stopped following us to Leonato's?
BENEDICK I would your grace would constrain me to tell.	**BENEDICK** I wish your grace would force me to tell you.
DON PEDRO I charge thee on thy allegiance.	**DON PEDRO** I order you as an act of loyalty to tell me.
BENEDICK You hear, Count Claudio: I can be secret as a dumb man; I would have you think so; but, on my allegiance, mark you this, on my allegiance. He is in love. With who? now that is your grace's part. Mark how short his answer is;--With Hero, Leonato's short daughter.	**BENEDICK** Listen, Count Claudio: I can keep secrets like a mute, I assure you; but my allegiance forces me to tell Don Pedro – this is a matter of loyalty. Claudio is in love. With whom? That's what your grace should ask. Notice how 'short' his answer is;--With Hero, Leonato's short daughter.
CLAUDIO If this were so, so were it uttered.	**CLAUDIO** If you say so.
BENEDICK Like the old tale, my lord: 'it is not so, nor 'twas not so, but, indeed, God forbid it should be so.'	**BENEDICK** Like that old story, my lord: where the defendant in a murder trial keeps denying his guilt until he's proved guilty!

Original	Modern
CLAUDIO If my passion change not shortly, God forbid it should be otherwise.	**CLAUDIO** Unless my feelings change soon, I have to admit it is true.
DON PEDRO Amen, if you love her; for the lady is very well worthy.	**DON PEDRO** That's great, if you love her; Hero is definitely worthy of your love.
CLAUDIO You speak this to fetch me in, my lord.	**CLAUDIO** You're only saying this to trick me, my lord.
DON PEDRO By my troth, I speak my thought.	**DON PEDRO** I swear, I that's my honest opinion.
CLAUDIO And, in faith, my lord, I spoke mine.	**CLAUDIO** And I swear I shared my honest opinion with Benedick: I love Hero.
BENEDICK And, by my two faiths and troths, my lord, I spoke mine.	**BENEDICK** And, *I* swear, my lord, I gave my honest opinion: I meant what I said.
CLAUDIO That I love her, I feel.	**CLAUDIO** I feel that I love her.
DON PEDRO That she is worthy, I know.	**DON PEDRO** I know that she's worthy.
BENEDICK That I neither feel how she should be loved nor know how she should be worthy, is the opinion that fire cannot melt out of me: I will die in it at the stake.	**BENEDICK** I *don't* feel how she should be loved nor know how she should be worth loving, and that is the opinion that fire can't melt out of me: you could burn me at the stake and I'd still think so.
DON PEDRO Thou wast ever an obstinate heretic in the despite of beauty.	**DON PEDRO** You never did believe in the power of beauty.
CLAUDIO And never could maintain his part but in the force of his will.	**CLAUDIO** And it took all his will power to stick to that view.
BENEDICK That a woman conceived me, I thank her; that she brought me up, I likewise give her most humble thanks: but that I will have a recheat winded in my forehead, or hang my bugle in an invisible baldrick, all women shall pardon me. Because I will not do them the wrong to mistrust any, I will do myself the right to trust none; and the fine is, for the which I may go the finer, I will live a bachelor.	**BENEDICK** I'm grateful that a woman conceived me, I thank her that she brought me up: but all women will have to forgive me for being unwilling to be their plaything – I won't be cheated on by a wife. Because I don't want to doubt and mistrust any woman, I'll just avoid them all. I will live as a bachelor – and the benefit is, I'll have more money for fine clothes.
DON PEDRO I shall see thee, ere I die, look pale with love.	**DON PEDRO** Before I die, I'll see you look pale with love.

BENEDICK With anger, with sickness, or with hunger, my lord, not with love: prove that ever I lose more blood with love than I will get again with drinking, pick out mine eyes with a ballad-maker's pen and hang me up at the door of a brothel-house for the sign of blind Cupid.	**BENEDICK** With anger, with illness, or with hunger maybe, my lord, but not sick with love. If you can prove that I'll ever be so in love that I can't be brought to my senses by a night in the pub, you can pluck out my eyes with a love-poet's pen and hang me up at the door of a brothel where the blind Cupid sign usually goes.
DON PEDRO Well, if ever thou dost fall from this faith, thou wilt prove a notable argument.	**DON PEDRO** Well, if you ever do fall in love, I'm sure everyone would be interested in hearing these promises.
BENEDICK If I do, hang me in a bottle like a cat and shoot at me; and he that hits me, let him be clapped on the shoulder, and called Adam.	**BENEDICK** If I do, use me for target practice and make a hero of everyone that hits me. Call them 'Adam Bell' after the famous archer.
DON PEDRO Well, as time shall try: 'In time the savage bull doth bear the yoke.'	**DON PEDRO** Well, we'll see. Remember the saying: 'In time the savage bull bears the yoke.'
BENEDICK The savage bull may; but if ever the sensible Benedick bear it, pluck off the bull's horns and set them in my forehead: and let me be vilely painted, and in such great letters as they write 'Here is good horse to hire,' let them signify under my sign 'Here you may see Benedick the married man.'	**BENEDICK** The savage bull may; but if ever the sensible Benedick is domesticated, you can put the bull's horns on my forehead, because any wife is sure to cheat on me. You might as well hang a big sign with huge lettering around my neck. Instead of saying 'Here is good horse to hire,' let is say, 'Here you may see Benedick the married man.'
CLAUDIO If this should ever happen, thou wouldst be horn-mad.	**CLAUDIO** If that should ever happen, you would go mad like a rutting buck.
DON PEDRO Nay, if Cupid have not spent all his quiver in Venice, thou wilt quake for this shortly.	**DON PEDRO** No, if Cupid hasn't used up all his arrows in Venice, I predict you will soon be quaking with love.
BENEDICK I look for an earthquake too, then.	**BENEDICK** I'll expect an earthquake too, then.
DON PEDRO Well, you temporize with the hours. In the meantime, good Signor Benedick, repair to Leonato's: commend me to him and tell him I will not fail him at supper; for indeed he hath made great preparation.	**DON PEDRO** Well, you'll soften in time. Meantime, good Sir Benedick, hurry to Leonato's: pay my respects and tell him I'll definitely be there for supper; I know he's gone to a lot of trouble to make it a feast.
BENEDICK I have almost matter enough in me for such an embassage; and so I commit you--	**BENEDICK** I think I should be able to manage that; and so I commit you--
CLAUDIO To the tuition of God: From my house, if I had it,--	**CLAUDIO** 'Into God's protection: From my house, if I had it-'

DON PEDRO The sixth of July: Your loving friend, Benedick.	**DON PEDRO** 'The sixth of July: Your loving friend, Benedick.'
BENEDICK Nay, mock not, mock not. The body of your discourse is sometime guarded with fragments, and the guards are but slightly basted on neither: ere you flout old ends any further, examine your conscience: and so I leave you.	**BENEDICK** Don't mock, don't mock. Sometimes you two weave fragments of wit into your conversation, but it weakens rather than improves it. Before you joke about me, look long and hard at yourself, examine your conscience: I'm going now
Exit	*Exit*
CLAUDIO My liege, your highness now may do me good.	**CLAUDIO** My lord, I'd appreciate your help with this.
DON PEDRO My love is thine to teach: teach it but how, And thou shalt see how apt it is to learn Any hard lesson that may do thee good.	**DON PEDRO** I'm at your service: just tell me how I can help and I'll do my best. No matter how difficult the favour, I'm eager to help.
CLAUDIO Hath Leonato any son, my lord?	**CLAUDIO** Does Leonato have a son, my lord?
DON PEDRO No child but Hero; she's his only heir. Dost thou affect her, Claudio?	**DON PEDRO** Hero is his only child; she's his only heir. Do you love her, Claudio?
CLAUDIO O, my lord, When you went onward on this ended action, I look'd upon her with a soldier's eye, That liked, but had a rougher task in hand Than to drive liking to the name of love: But now I am return'd and that war-thoughts Have left their places vacant, in their rooms Come thronging soft and delicate desires, All prompting me how fair young Hero is, Saying, I liked her ere I went to wars.	**CLAUDIO** O, my lord, when left Messina to fight the war just over, I looked at her with a soldier's eye. I liked what I saw, but my attention was on the violent battle ahead, so I couldn't allow liking to become love. But now that I'm back, thoughts of war have receded, leaving space for the soft, delicate feelings of love, making me notice how beautiful young Hero is, reminding me why I liked her before I went to war.
DON PEDRO Thou wilt be like a lover presently And tire the hearer with a book of words. If thou dost love fair Hero, cherish it, And I will break with her and with her father, And thou shalt have her. Was't not to this end That thou began'st to twist so fine a story?	**DON PEDRO** You'll soon be like a true lover exhausting everyone with endless discussions of love. If you *do* love beautiful Hero, treasure it; I'll negotiate with her and with her father, persuading Leonarto to let you have Hero. Isn't that the reason you told me all this?
CLAUDIO How sweetly you do minister to love, That know love's grief by his complexion! But lest my liking might too sudden seem, I would have salved it with a longer treatise.	**CLAUDIO** You know just how to care for the love-sick! But I'm worried that I might seem over hasty in my emotions. Shall I explain the whole story, to you and to them?
DON PEDRO What need the bridge much broader than the flood? The fairest grant is the necessity. Look, what will serve is fit: 'tis once, thou lovest,	**DON PEDRO** Why speak longer than you have to? A bridge goes directly across even a flooded river. Whatever gets the job done is enough.

And I will fit thee with the remedy. I know we shall have revelling to-night: I will assume thy part in some disguise And tell fair Hero I am Claudio, And in her bosom I'll unclasp my heart And take her hearing prisoner with the force And strong encounter of my amorous tale: Then after to her father will I break; And the conclusion is, she shall be thine. In practise let us put it presently. *Exeunt*	Look, I only need to know that you love Hero to find a solution to your problem. Now, I know we'll have a masked ball to-night: I'll disguise myself as you and tell Hero that I am Claudio, and pour out 'my' loving feelings so persuasively that she'll be captured by love. Then I'll negotiate with her father, Leonarto; And the conclusion is, she'll be your wife. So, let's get started right away. *They both exit.*

Analysis of Act 1 Scene 1

In this scene we meet the main characters and become aware of the themes the play will explore.

Summary:
When a messenger brings Leonarto news that Don Pedro and his army are coming to stay with him, he reports that one of the noblemen, Count Claudio, has stood out as a brave soldier. Beatrice questions the messenger about Benedick, all the while insulting him, so Leonarto explains that there is a 'merry war' between them.

The men arrive and Don Pedro praises Leonarto for his hospitality and, noticing Hero, asks whether she is Leonarto's daughter. Benedick uses the opportunity to joke about her legitimacy using double meanings. Beatrice sneers that no one is listening to Benedick, which leads to a 'merry war' of words. They trade insults for a while, then Benedick says he's had enough and walks away, leaving Beatrice fuming that he has had the last word as usual.

As the prince [Don Pedro] and Leonarto go inside with everyone else, Claudio asks Benedick what he thinks of Hero. It becomes clear that he wants to marry her, a thought that disgusts the confirmed bachelor, Benedick.

Returning to see what is keeping the two, Don Pedro predicts that he will see Benedick fall in love one day and, after sending Benedick off on an errand so that they can talk, promises to help Claudio win Hero at the masked ball that night.

Title:
Much Ado About Nothing literally means 'a lot of fuss about something insignificant', so as you read the play, be on the alert for things that seem to be important but turn out to be 'no big deal'- we'll discuss examples as we come across them.

There are other interpretations of the title: 'nothing' and 'noting' were apparently homophones in Shakespeare's day. 'Noting' used to mean chiefly gossiping, overhearing things, circulating rumours: think of it as 'hot news'. So notice how many times letters, notes, notices, taking note- as in spying and eavesdropping- and outward show – something 'of note' – are foregrounded. Musical notation is also referred to in Balthazar's speech: 'Note this before my notes/There's not a note of mine that's worth the noting' as well as the songs and references to music.

Genre:
Shakespeare explores love in this **romantic comedy** and in Scene 1 we see two types of love. Claudio is everything an Elizabethan nobleman was meant to be: honorable, a brave soldier, someone who made his family proud. In fact, his uncle was so delighted by the good reputation Claudio earned he burst into tears at the news of his valor. Hero is his female counterpart: a wealthy heiress, beautiful and meek – she has hardly said a word so far (one sentence). Notice throughout the play how little she speaks in comparison to Beatrice. In fact, she has the fewest lines of the four main characters. What she *doesn't* say is almost more noteworthy than what she does say: she seems to have no opinions, is never critical and never angry. You could say she's more of an ideal than a real person.

So on the one hand we have Hero and Claudio (notice both names end in 'o', perhaps suggesting they're not quite so great after all?) as the ideal couple with the 'fairytale love'.
Beatrice and Benedick (both names begin with a plosive 'B') on the other hand, are far from ideal. They are both too opinionated, argumentative and determined not to be hurt by love. Beatrice

particularly refuses to conform to the role of obedient companion assigned to women in the patriarchal society, where men were in charge and women were their possessions.

Context:
Shakespeare himself didn't conform to the norms of his time when it came to love.
Because marriage was more like a business transaction (notice Claudio asking whether Leonarto has a son, to check who'll get the money!), Shakespeare should have consulted his father, then together they would have negotiated with his younger bride's family- a bit like Don Pedro will do for Claudio ... but what actually happened was that he fell in love with a 26 year old when he was only 18. Ann Hathaway was fairly independent and though she lived with her brother, she owned her own land. Remember, Shakespeare was not famous at the time, nor was he rich: not much of a catch. Germaine Greer suggests that both families would probably have been against the marriage and so to make it happen the couple decided to have a baby, which meant they had to get married before the child was born to save it from being illegitimate.

Themes:

- Relationships

The relationship Shakespeare explores in Beatrice and Benedick is a much more modern one than the Elizabethan ideal. They know each other, 'warts and all'. Their 'merry war' ensures that they notice and talk to each other at every opportunity.

Despite disguising it as a chance to be insulting about him, notice that Beatrice is actually trying to get information about Benedick from the messenger. Has he returned safely? Was he brave? Who is his friend?

Claudio had merely looked at Hero 'with a soldier's eye,/That liked, but had a rougher task in hand/Than to drive liking to the name of love', but Beatrice says she had promised Benedick 'to eat all of his killing', which suggests they'd definitely been at each other before the soldiers left for war. The pre-existing relationship is confirmed later in the scene when Beatrice says 'I know you of old', meaning she knows all his tricks from before. In Act 2 you'll discover a bit more about their former relationship, but for now it is worth noticing how paranoid Benedick is about being cheated on. He calls Beatrice 'Lady Disdain', suggesting she is always putting him down, scorning him. Again in Act 2 you'll see more of the effect her scornful attitude has on him.

The real give-away of course is Benedick's verdict that Beatrice is actually much more beautiful than Hero: 'there's her cousin, an she were not possessed with a fury, exceeds her as much in beauty as the first of May doth the last of December'.

Language
Shakespeare loves to play with words and uses puns and double meanings throughout the play. For example, when Beatrice says:' Is it possible disdain should die when she hath such meet food to feed it...' the word 'meet' means 'suitable', but it's a pun on 'meat' as well, linking with the idea of food to eat. The animal imagery in their 'slanging match' suggests that despite their 'witty' veneer, the insults Beatrice and Benedick hurl at each other are expressing very basic emotions. On the other hand, Claudio calls Hero a 'jewel', claiming 'In mine eye she is the sweetest lady that ever I looked on' and 'I look'd upon her with a soldier's eye,/That liked' – all suggest infatuation, rather than love based on knowing each other. He even leaves wooing her [chatting her up] to Don Pedro! He seems more in love with the idea of being in love than with Hero: Shakespeare suggests that he is playing a role when Don Pedro says, 'Thou wilt be like a lover presently,/ And tire the hearer with a book of words', also suggesting that he has been twisting a fine story – or manipulating the conversation – to get Don Pedro to agree to broker the deal in his name.

Act 1 Scene 2

ORIGINAL TEXT	MODERN TRANSLATION
A room in LEONATO's house.	**A room in LEONATO's house.**
Enter LEONATO and ANTONIO, meeting	*Enter LEONATO and ANTONIO, meeting*
LEONATO How now, brother! Where is my cousin, your son? Hath he provided this music?	**LEONATO** Hi there, brother! Where is my nephew, your son? Has he taken care of the music?
ANTONIO He is very busy about it. But, brother, I can tell you strange news that you yet dreamt not of.	**ANTONIO** He's busy with it right now. But, I've got some strange news for you, brother, that you'd never have dreamt of.
LEONATO Are they good?	**LEONATO** Is it good news?
ANTONIO As the event stamps them: but they have a good cover; they show well outward. The prince and Count Claudio, walking in a thick-pleached alley in mine orchard, were thus much overheard by a man of mine: the prince discovered to Claudio that he loved my niece your daughter and meant to acknowledge it this night in a dance: and if he found her accordant, he meant to take the present time by the top and instantly break with you of it.	**ANTONIO** On the face of it. My servant overheard the prince and Count Claudio while they were taking a walk in my orchard. The prince told Claudio that he loved Hero, your daughter, and meant to tell so her at dance tonight. If she shared his feelings, he was planning to ask you there and then for her hand in marriage.
LEONATO Hath the fellow any wit that told you this?	**LEONATO** And this servant of yours would have got it right?
ANTONIO A good sharp fellow: I will send for him; and question him yourself.	**ANTONIO** He's a bright chap! I call for him, and you can ask him yourself.
LEONATO No, no; we will hold it as a dream till it appear itself: but I will acquaint my daughter withal, that she may be the better prepared for an answer, if peradventure this be true. Go you and tell her of it.	**LEONATO** No, no; we'll just treat it like a dream until it actually happens. But I will let Hero know, so she's got time to think about her answer if it turns out to be true. Will you tell her for me?
Enter Attendants	*Enter Attendants*
Cousins, you know what you have to do. O, I cry you mercy, friend; go you with me, and I will use your skill. Good cousin, have a care this busy time.	OK chaps, you know what you have to do. Ah, my friend; you come with me, I could use your skill. Dear cousin, be careful during this busy time.
Exeunt	*They all exit*

Analysis of Act 1 Scene 2

This is like a game of 'Chinese Whispers': in this scene the very conversation we've just heard between Claudio and Don Pedro is wrongly reported – first by a servant to Antonio, then by Antonio to his brother Leonarto, Hero's father – as Don Pedro's confession of love.

Summary:
Leonarto is busy checking that everything is being organised for the party that evening. His brother Antonio reports that a servant overheard Don Pedro tell Claudio he loves Hero and will ask her to marry his that evening at the party. Leonarto asks Antonio to prepare Hero for this so that she knows what to reply.

Genre:
One of the characteristics of comedy is that things get muddled through this kind of misunderstanding. Because the audience knows what was really said, we anticipate the mix-up that could be caused by Hero thinking it is actually Don Pedro that wants to marry her.

Context:
Don Pedro is a prince, while Claudio is a Count. When Antonio says 'I can tell you strange news that you yet dreamt not of' it is because a match between Hero and Don Pedro would mean significant social advancement for Hero. Leonarto doesn't quite believe it and although he thinks Hero should be warned, just in case it is true, he says it's better to pretend it's a dream until it is proved true.

Themes:

- Marriage

For most of history the only career open to a woman of the upper class was marriage: Making a socially and financially advantageous marriage was too important to be influenced by love or to be left to the woman to decide on; fathers, uncles and brothers were the ones to arrange a suitable match.

Language
Read the end of Act1 scene1 again, from 'I know we shall have revelling to-night:' to 'In practise let us put it presently.' Notice how the words '...tell fair Hero *I am Claudio'* have been missed by the eavesdropper, leading to the misinterpretation that 'the prince discovered [revealed] to Claudio that he loved my niece your daughter and meant to acknowledge [admit/ confess] it this night in a dance: and if he found her accordant [willing to agree], he meant to take the present time by the top and instantly break with you of it.'

Act 1 Scene 3

ORIGINAL TEXT	MODERN TRANSLATION
The same.	**The same place.**
Enter DON JOHN and CONRADE	*Enter DON JOHN and CONRADE*
CONRADE What the good-year, my lord! why are you thus out of measure sad?	**CONRADE** Really, my lord! Why are you so unduly sad?
DON JOHN There is no measure in the occasion that breeds; therefore the sadness is without limit.	**DON JOHN** There's no limit to the things that cause my sadness, so there's no limit to my sadness.
CONRADE You should hear reason.	**CONRADE** You should listen to reason.
DON JOHN And when I have heard it, what blessing brings it?	**DON JOHN** And when I've listened, how will I be better off?
CONRADE If not a present remedy, at least a patient sufferance.	**CONRADE** If it doesn't put an end to it, at least it will help you put up with it.
DON JOHN I wonder that thou, being, as thou sayest thou art, born under Saturn, goest about to apply a moral medicine to a mortifying mischief. I cannot hide what I am: I must be sad when I have cause and smile at no man's jests, eat when I have stomach and wait for no man's leisure, sleep when I am drowsy and tend on no man's business, laugh when I am merry and claw no man in his humour.	**DON JOHN** I'm amazed that someone who admits to being born under the moody influence of Saturn, thinks there's a quick moral cure for a deadly disease. I can't hide what I am: if I'm sad, I'll be sad, and I won't smile at anyone's jokes; I'll eat when I'm hungry, not when it's convenient for others, sleep when I'm sleepy and not rouse myself to attend to anybody's business. I'll laugh when I'm happy, not to butter anyone up.
CONRADE Yea, but you must not make the full show of this till you may do it without controlment. You have of late stood out against your brother, and he hath ta'en you newly into his grace; where it is impossible you should take true root but by the fair weather that you make yourself: it is needful that you frame the season for your own harvest.	**CONRADE** Yes, but rein it in a bit until it's safe. It's not long since you were fighting against your brother, and he's only just forgiven you; but you still need to smooth your own way back into his good books: once you're there, then you can have what you want.
DON JOHN I had rather be a canker in a hedge than a rose in his grace, and it better fits my blood to be disdained of all than to fashion a carriage to rob love from any: in this, though I cannot be said to be a flattering honest man, it must not be denied but I am a plain-dealing villain. I am trusted with a muzzle and enfranchised with a clog; therefore I have decreed not to sing in my cage.	**DON JOHN** I'd rather be a dog-rose in a hedge than a cultivated rose in his garden, and I'd rather be hated by everybody than smarm them into loving me. I might not be a charmer, but at least you know where you stand with me. My brother trusts me as long as I'm muzzled and gives me freedom to go as long as my feet are weighted down; but I won't be like a songbird in a cage.

If I had my mouth, I would bite; if I had my liberty, I would do my liking: in the meantime let me be that I am and seek not to alter me.	If I were really free, I could truly do as I pleased, but until then, let me be what I am, and don't try to change me.
CONRADE Can you make no use of your discontent?	**CONRADE** Can't you use your discontent to your advantage somehow?
DON JOHN I make all use of it, for I use it only. Who comes here?	**DON JOHN** It's all I do use, because it's all I have. Who's that?
Enter BORACHIO	*Enter BORACHIO*
What news, Borachio?	What's the news, Borachio?
BORACHIO I came yonder from a great supper: the prince your brother is royally entertained by Leonato: and I can give you intelligence of an intended marriage.	**BORACHIO** I've just come from a great feast which Leonato has put on for your brother, the Prince: and the news is of an intended marriage.
DON JOHN Will it serve for any model to build mischief on? What is he for a fool that betroths himself to unquietness?	**DON JOHN** Is this a chance to make mischief? Who's the fool that's looking for trouble and strife?
BORACHIO Marry, it is your brother's right hand.	**BORACHIO-** It's your brother's right-hand man.
DON JOHN Who? the most exquisite Claudio?	**DON JOHN** What? The lovely Claudio?
BORACHIO Even he.	**BORACHIO** The very same.
DON JOHN A proper squire! And who, and who? which way looks he?	**DON JOHN** He's a fine one! And who is it he's got his eye on?
BORACHIO Marry, on Hero, the daughter and heir of Leonato.	**BORACHIO** Hero, Leonato's daughter and heir
DON JOHN A very forward March-chick! How came you to this?	**DON JOHN** A little madam! How did you find this out?
BORACHIO Being entertained for a perfumer, as I was smoking a musty room, comes me the prince and Claudio, hand in hand in sad conference: I whipt me behind the arras; and there heard it agreed upon that the prince should woo Hero for himself, and having obtained her, give her to Count Claudio.	**BORACHIO** I was employed to perfume Leonato's house, and I was working in a particularly musty room, the Prince and Claudio appeared, talking earnestly: I quickly hid behind a wall-hanging from where I overheard them agree that the Prince should woo Hero as if for himself but, having won her, hand her over to Count Claudio.
DON JOHN Come, come, let us thither: this may prove food to my displeasure. That young start-up hath all the	**DON JOHN** Come, let's go to the dance: this may be just what I need. That young upstart Claudio was responsible

glory of my overthrow: if I can cross him any way, I bless myself every way. You are both sure, and will assist me?	for my downfall: if I can do anything to cross him, it'll make me very happy. You're both with me, I take it?
CONRADE To the death, my lord.	**CONRADE** Until our dying breath, my lord.
DON JOHN Let us to the great supper: their cheer is the greater that I am subdued. Would the cook were of my mind! Shall we go prove what's to be done?	**DON JOHN** Let's go to the feast, then: they're only too happy to see me in this subdued state. It's a pity the cook doesn't think like me -they'd have a rough night! Let's go and suss out the scene?
BORACHIO We'll wait upon your lordship.	**BORACHIO** We're right behind your lordship.
Exeunt	*They all exit*

Analysis of Act 1 Scene 3

Here the conversation between Don Pedro and Claudio is correctly reported and the audience told that mischief is planned.

Summary:
Don John has been going about with a long face and his companion Conrad warns him at least to pretend to be reconciled to his brother Don Pedro, who has forgiven him for the rebellion he organised. He is being spiteful and nasty at every opportunity, which is too obvious – if he wants to do mischief he has to be subtle about it, Conrad tells him. Don John insists he can, he is a 'a plain-dealing villain'. Then Borachio arrives with the news that Don Pedro will win Hero on Claudio's behalf. Immediately they vow to turn this into an opportunity to do harm to Claudio.

Context:
Don John is also called 'the bastard' in the play – this is not swearing as it would be today, to Shakespeare's audience it meant that he was 'illegitimate', born to parents who weren't married. It is probable that he is older than Don Pedro and feels that he should have inherited the kingdom and has now tried to take it forcibly through war.

At the start of the Act we heard how well Claudio had fought and here we hear that he had 'all the glory of my overthrow', so was instrumental in Don John's downfall.

Themes:

- Loyalty and disloyalty

Since his defeat, Don John has been on the lookout for ways in which to undermine his brother. Conrad says he should feign [fake] loyalty in order to be able to do mischief, but he insists:' let me be that I am, and seek not to alter me'. When Barachio brings the news of Claudio's love for Hero, he immediately plans to avenge himself on both his brother and his brother's great favourite, Claudio, by doing something villainous [wicked]

Structure:
This scene is in two parts, the first being a character sketch of Don John. We can infer that he is proud of being so 'plain-dealing' a villain by the way he insists on being as he is. Conrad wants him to seem reconciled until an opportunity arises to do mischief and it does when Barachio enters with the news. The second half of the scene is then devoted to hearing the news and deciding to use it wickedly. Notice that Barachio is reporting the conversation between Don Pedro and Claudio correctly, but intends to subvert it. So Shakespeare is building up to two potential disasters: the wrong message believed and the right message subverted [undermined].

Language:
Conrad uses nature imagery: 'take true root', 'make fair weather', 'frame the season for your own harvest' and Don John briefly does the same in his reply, 'I had rather be a canker in a hedge than a rose in his grace'. Perhaps this is how Shakespeare emphasises that Don John really is a villain – he is not going to turn into a good guy – in Act 2 it is really important that we remember that.

Act 2 Scene 1

ORIGINAL TEXT	MODERN TRANSLATION
A hall in LEONATO'S house.	**A hall in LEONATO'S house.**
Enter LEONATO, ANTONIO, HERO, BEATRICE, and others	*Enter LEONATO, ANTONIO, HERO, BEATRICE, and others*
LEONATO Was not Count John here at supper?	**LEONATO** Wasn't Don John here for dinner?
ANTONIO I saw him not.	**ANTONIO** I didn't see him.
BEATRICE How tartly that gentleman looks! I never can see him but I am heart-burned an hour after.	**BEATRICE** That man is so sour looking! I can't even look at him without getting heartburn.
HERO He is of a very melancholy disposition.	**HERO** He's a real old misery-guts to look at.
BEATRICE He were an excellent man that were made just in the midway between him and Benedick: the one is too like an image and says nothing, and the other too like my lady's eldest son, evermore tattling.	**BEATRICE** What you want is somebody half-way between Don John and Benedick: one of them is more like a picture of a man - he never speaks - and the other like a spoiled brat who never stops babbling.
LEONATO Then half Signior Benedick's tongue in Count John's mouth, and half Count John's melancholy in Signior Benedick's face,--	**LEONATO** So he'd talk only half as much as Benedick and be only half as serious as Don John...
BEATRICE With a good leg and a good foot, uncle, and money enough in his purse, such a man would win any woman in the world, if a' could get her good-will.	**BEATRICE** And if he was a good dancer, and had plenty of money, such a man could have any woman he wanted, with a little good will from her.
LEONATO By my troth, niece, thou wilt never get thee a husband, if thou be so shrewd of thy tongue.	**LEONATO** Honestly, niece, you'll never get a husband if you keep saying such nasty things about people.
ANTONIO In faith, she's too curst.	**ANTONIO** It's true: she's too bad-tempered.
BEATRICE Too curst is more than curst: I shall lessen God's sending that way; for it is said, 'God sends a curst cow short horns;' but to a cow too curst he sends none.	**BEATRICE** So too bad-tempered is worse than bad-tempered, right?: So if, as the proverb says, God gives a bad-tempered cow short horns so it can do less damage, then surely he gives a too bad tempered cow no horns at all!
LEONATO So, by being too curst, God will send you no horns.	**LEONATO** You mean because you're so bad-tempered, God will give you no horns, so you can do less damage?

BEATRICE
Just, if he send me no husband; for the which blessing I am at him upon my knees every morning and evening. Lord, I could not endure a husband with a beard on his face: I had rather lie in the woollen.

LEONATO
You may light on a husband that hath no beard.

BEATRICE
What should I do with him? dress him in my apparel and make him my waiting-gentlewoman? He that hath a beard is more than a youth, and he that hath no beard is less than a man: and he that is more than a youth is not for me, and he that is less than a man, I am not for him: therefore, I will even take sixpence in earnest of the bear-ward, and lead his apes into hell.

LEONATO
Well, then, go you into hell?

BEATRICE
No, but to the gate; and there will the devil meet me, like an old cuckold, with horns on his head, and say 'Get you to heaven, Beatrice, get you to heaven; here's no place for you maids:' so deliver I up my apes, and away to Saint Peter for the heavens; he shows me where the bachelors sit, and there live we as merry as the day is long.

ANTONIO
[To HERO] Well, niece, I trust you will be ruled by your father.

BEATRICE
Yes, faith; it is my cousin's duty to make curtsy and say 'Father, as it please you.' But yet for all that, cousin, let him be a handsome fellow, or else make another curtsy and say 'Father, as it please me.'

LEONATO
Well, niece, I hope to see you one day fitted with a husband.

BEATRICE
Not till God make men of some other metal than earth. Would it not grieve a woman to be overmastered with a piece of valiant dust? to make an account of her life to a clod of wayward marl? No, uncle, I'll none: Adam's sons are my brethren; and, truly, I hold it a sin to match in my kindred.

BEATRICE
Precisely! Indeed I pray every morning and evening that God won't give me a husband. I couldn't stand a husband with a beard - I'd rather sleep in itchy blankets all night.

LEONATO
Maybe you'll find a husband without a beard.

BEATRICE
What should I do with a husband like that? Dress him in my clothes and make him my maid? If he's got a beard he is more than a boy, and if he hasn't then he's less than a man. But if he's more than a boy he's not my type, and he's less than a man, I'm not his. So, it looks like I'm going to suffer the fate of an unmarried woman, as the saying goes, and 'lead the apes to hell'.

LEONATO
So you're going to hell, then?
BEATRICE
No, only to the gate, where I'll be met by the devil, with horns on his head, like a cuckold, and he'll say 'Go off to heaven, Beatrice, we don't take virgins here!' So I'll deliver my apes, and go off to heaven to find Saint Peter - and he'll show me where all the bachelors hang out, and we'll all live happily ever after.

ANTONIO
[To HERO] Well, niece, I hope you will do what your father says.

BEATRICE
It is indeed my cousin's duty to say 'as you wish, Father' - but all the same, if her father's choice of husband isn't handsome, she should politely say 'no, Father, as I wish!'

LEONATO
Well, niece, I hope I will see you married one day.
BEATRICE
Not until God makes men out of something better than dust, like it says in the Bible, I won't. What woman would want to be lorded over by handful of dust? to answer to a lump of clay? No, uncle, it's not for me: and anyway, if Adam is the father of all mankind then his sons are my brothers, and surely marrying your own brother is wrong?

LEONATO Daughter, remember what I told you: if the prince do solicit you in that kind, you know your answer.	**LEONATO** [to Hero] Daughter, remember what I told you: if the Prince does ask you to marry him, you know what answer to give him.
BEATRICE The fault will be in the music, cousin, if you be not wooed in good time: if the prince be too important, tell him there is measure in every thing and so dance out the answer. For, hear me, Hero: wooing, wedding, and repenting, is as a Scotch jig, a measure, and a cinque pace: the first suit is hot and hasty, like a Scotch jig, and full as fantastical; the wedding, mannerly-modest, as a measure, full of state and ancientry; and then comes repentance and, with his bad legs, falls into the cinque pace faster and faster, till he sink into his grave.	**BEATRICE** Make sure the Prince woos you properly, cousin: if he tries to rush you, tell him that he must see courting as a sort of dance. Listen carefully to me Hero: there are three stages in a relationship, and they are each like different dances. The wooing is hot and breathless like a Scottish jig, just as hasty, and just as full of wild ideas; the wedding is a stately dance, full of old-fashioned formality; and then comes the bit where you regret getting married, which is like a five-step capering dance what whirls you round faster and faster until you collapse and die.
LEONATO Cousin, you apprehend passing shrewdly.	**LEONATO** Niece, you are very perceptive.
BEATRICE I have a good eye, uncle; I can see a church by daylight.	**BEATRICE** I have good eyes, uncle; I can see what's plain to see.
LEONATO The revellers are entering, brother: make good room.	**LEONATO** The partygoers have arrived, brother: we must make room for them
All put on their masks *Enter DON PEDRO, CLAUDIO, BENEDICK, BALTHASAR, DON JOHN, BORACHIO, MARGARET, URSULA and others, masked*	*All put on their masks* *Enter DON PEDRO, CLAUDIO, BENEDICK, BALTHASAR, DON JOHN, BORACHIO, MARGARET, URSULA and others enter, wearing masks.*
DON PEDRO Lady, will you walk about with your friend?	**DON PEDRO** Lady, will you dance with me?
HERO So you walk softly and look sweetly and say nothing, I am yours for the walk; and especially when I walk away.	**HERO** As long as you move well, look good and don't talk too much, I am yours for this dance; maybe even after I leave the floor
DON PEDRO With me in your company?	**DON PEDRO** Shall I leave with you?
HERO I may say so, when I please.	**HERO** I might decide to let you.
DON PEDRO And when please you to say so?	**DON PEDRO** And when will that be?
HERO When I like your favour; for God defend the lute should be like the case!	**HERO** When I decide I like your appearance; but God help you if you're as ugly as your mask!

DON PEDRO My visor is Philemon's roof; within the house is Jove.	**DON PEDRO** My mask is like the roof of Philemon's humble cottage, under which the god Jove is disguised.
HERO Why, then, your visor should be thatched.	**HERO** Perhaps then your mask should be thatched like her cottage.
DON PEDRO Speak low, if you speak love.	**DON PEDRO** If you're speaking words of love, speak softly.
Drawing her aside	*He leads her aside. The focus changes to BALTHASAR and MARGARET*
BALTHASAR Well, I would you did like me.	**BALTHASAR** I wish you liked me.
MARGARET So would not I, for your own sake; for I have many ill-qualities.	**MARGARET** You're lucky I don't; I've got a lot of bad habits
BALTHASAR Which is one?	**BALTHASAR** Name one?
MARGARET I say my prayers aloud.	**MARGARET** I say my prayers out loud.
BALTHASAR I love you the better: the hearers may cry, Amen.	**BALTHASAR** That makes me love you even more: all those who hear can shout Amen to them!
MARGARET God match me with a good dancer!	**MARGARET** God give me a good dance partner!
BALTHASAR Amen.	**BALTHASAR** That's me! Amen!
MARGARET And God keep him out of my sight when the dance is done! Answer, clerk.	**MARGARET** And God keep him away from me when the dance is over! Say Amen to that one!
BALTHASAR No more words: the clerk is answered.	**BALTHASAR** Enough said: I've got my answer.
	The focus changes to URSULA and ANTONIO
URSULA I know you well enough; you are Signior Antonio.	**URSULA** I know who you are; you're Signior Antonio.
ANTONIO At a word, I am not.	**ANTONIO** No, really, I'm not.
URSULA I know you by the waggling of your head.	**URSULA** I recognise you by the way your head waggles.
ANTONIO To tell you true, I counterfeit him.	**ANTONIO** Really, no - I'm just pretending to be him.

URSULA You could never do him so ill-well, unless you were the very man. Here's his dry hand up and down: you are he, you are he.	**URSULA** Nobody could imitate his imperfections so well if they weren't him. You've got exactly the same wrinkly hands: you are definitely him!
ANTONIO At a word, I am not.	**ANTONIO** Well, I say I'm not.
URSULA Come, come, do you think I do not know you by your excellent wit? can virtue hide itself? Go to, mum, you are he: graces will appear, and there's an end.	**URSULA** Come on, you think I don't recognise you by your quick wits? can good things hide themselves? Shush now - I know you're Antonio: a person's virtues will always shine through and that's that. *They move aside.* ***BENEDICK*** *and* ***BEATRICE*** *move forward.*
BEATRICE Will you not tell me who told you so?	**BEATRICE** Won't you tell me who told you that?
BENEDICK No, you shall pardon me.	**BENEDICK** You must forgive me, but no.
BEATRICE Nor will you not tell me who you are?	**BEATRICE** And you won't tell me who you are either?
BENEDICK Not now.	**BENEDICK** Not now.
BEATRICE That I was disdainful, and that I had my good wit out of the 'Hundred Merry Tales:'--well this was Signior Benedick that said so.	**BEATRICE** Who was it who said I sneered at everyone, and that I got all my good lines out of a joke book? I bet it was Sir Benedick, wasn't it?
BENEDICK What's he?	**BENEDICK** Who's he?
BEATRICE I am sure you know him well enough.	**BEATRICE** I 'm sure you know him well enough.
BENEDICK Not I, believe me.	**BENEDICK** Believe me, I don't!
BEATRICE Did he never make you laugh?	**BEATRICE** Did he never make you laugh?
BENEDICK I pray you, what is he?	**BENEDICK** Please tell me, who is he?
BEATRICE Why, he is the prince's jester: a very dull fool; only his gift is in devising impossible slanders: none but libertines delight in him; and the commendation is not in his wit, but in his villany; for he both pleases men and angers them, and then	**BEATRICE** Why, he's the Prince's court jester: he's not very funny, though; all he's good at is making up unbelievable slanders about people: only the worst people think he's funny and even then only for his grossness, not his wit; he amuses people but also annoys them, so they both laugh at him and slap

they laugh at him and beat him. I am sure he is in the fleet: I would he had boarded me.	him. I am sure he's at this dance: I half wish he'd come up to me.
BENEDICK When I know the gentleman, I'll tell him what you say.	**BENEDICK** When I meet this gentleman, I'll tell him what you say.
BEATRICE Do, do: he'll but break a comparison or two on me; which, peradventure not marked or not laughed at, strikes him into melancholy; and then there's a partridge wing saved, for the fool will eat no supper that night.	**BEATRICE** Please do. He's bound to try to slag me off, but if nobody pays him any attention, as they probably won't, he'll get really grumpy and not want to eat; which will mean there's one more partridge wing for the rest of us.
Music	*Music for the dance begins*
We must follow the leaders.	Come, we must follow the dance leaders.
BENEDICK In every good thing.	**BENEDICK** Wherever they go.
BEATRICE Nay, if they lead to any ill, I will leave them at the next turning.	**BEATRICE** No, if they lead to harm, I will leave them at the first opportunity.
Dance. Then exeunt all except DON JOHN, BORACHIO, and CLAUDIO	*The dance starts. Then everyone except DON JOHN, BORACHIO, and CLAUDIO exits.*
DON JOHN Sure my brother is amorous on Hero and hath withdrawn her father to break with him about it. The ladies follow her and but one visor remains.	**DON JOHN** My brother is certainly keen on Hero and he's just taken her father aside to let him know his intentions. The ladies have gone off with Hero, but there's one masked man left there.
BORACHIO And that is Claudio: I know him by his bearing.	**BORACHIO** And that's Claudio: I recognise him by the way he carries himself.
DON JOHN Are not you Signior Benedick?	**DON JOHN** (*to* Claudio) Aren't you Sir Benedick?
CLAUDIO You know me well; I am he.	**CLAUDIO** You know me too well; that's me.
DON JOHN Signior, you are very near my brother in his love: he is enamoured on Hero; I pray you, dissuade him from her: she is no equal for his birth: you may do the part of an honest man in it.	**DON JOHN** Sir, my brother is very fond of you. He's in love with Hero; please make him change his mind: she's too low-born to marry a Prince. You'd be doing the right thing.
CLAUDIO How know you he loves her?	**CLAUDIO** How do you know that he loves her?
DON JOHN I heard him swear his affection.	**DON JOHN** I heard him swear his love.

BORACHIO So did I too; and he swore he would marry her to-night.	**BORACHIO** I heard it too; and he swore he would marry her to-night.
DON JOHN Come, let us to the banquet.	**DON JOHN** Come, let's get to the banquet.
Exeunt DON JOHN and BORACHIO	*DON JOHN and BORACHIO both leave*
CLAUDIO Thus answer I in the name of Benedick, But hear these ill news with the ears of Claudio. 'Tis certain so; the prince woos for himself. Friendship is constant in all other things Save in the office and affairs of love. Therefore, all hearts in love use their own tongues; Let every eye negotiate for itself And trust no agent; for beauty is a witch Against whose charms faith melteth into blood. This is an accident of hourly proof, Which I mistrusted not. Farewell, therefore, Hero!	**CLAUDIO** *(taking off his mask)* Though I was answering in Benedick's name, I heard this bad news with the ears of Claudio. So that's the Prince's game; he's courting Hero for himself, not me. You can rely on friends in everything, except when it comes to love. Lovers should always do their own courting, not rely on somebody else. Promises count for nothing when one is bewitched by beauty. It happens all the time. I should have expected it. So goodbye Hero!
Re-enter BENEDICK	*BENEDICK re-enters*
BENEDICK Count Claudio?	**BENEDICK** Count Claudio?
CLAUDIO Yea, the same.	**CLAUDIO** Yes, that's me.
BENEDICK Come, will you go with me?	**BENEDICK** Will you come with me?
CLAUDIO Whither?	**CLAUDIO** Where to?
BENEDICK Even to the next willow, about your own business, county. What fashion will you wear the garland of? about your neck, like an usurer's chain? or under your arm, like a lieutenant's scarf? You must wear it one way, for the prince hath got your Hero.	**BENEDICK** Well, a willow stands for unrequited love, so that's the place you need to go – how will you wear the garland you make? How about round your neck like a moneylender's chain, or maybe like a lieutenant's sash? But wear it you must, because the Prince has got your Hero.
CLAUDIO I wish him joy of her.	**CLAUDIO** I hope he is very happy with her.
BENEDICK Why, that's spoken like an honest drovier: so they sell bullocks. But did you think the prince would have served you thus?	**BENEDICK** You sound like a cattle dealer - as if you were just selling a bullock. Do you think the Prince would have behaved that way towards you?
CLAUDIO I pray you, leave me.	**CLAUDIO** Please, leave me alone.

BENEDICK Ho! now you strike like the blind man: 'twas the boy that stole your meat, and you'll beat the post.	**BENEDICK** Ha! Now your behaving like a blind man, thrashing a wooden post instead of the boy who stole your meat.
CLAUDIO If it will not be, I'll leave you.	**CLAUDIO** If you're not going to leave me, I'll leave you.
Exit	*He exits*
BENEDICK Alas, poor hurt fowl! now will he creep into sedges. But that my Lady Beatrice should know me, and not know me! The prince's fool! Ha? It may be I go under that title because I am merry. Yea, but so I am apt to do myself wrong; I am not so reputed: it is the base, though bitter, disposition of Beatrice that puts the world into her person and so gives me out. Well, I'll be revenged as I may.	**BENEDICK** Poor wounded bird! Now he creeps into the rough grass to hide... It's strange that Lady Beatrice should seem to know who I was yet not know who I was! 'The Prince's fool', eh? Maybe I'm called that because I'm so fun-loving. But I'm not being fair on myself; that's not the way people see me. It's Beatrice's mean, sarcastic nature that makes her think she speaks for everybody in what she says about me. Well, I'll get my revenge one way or another.
Re-enter DON PEDRO	*DON PEDRO re-enters*
DON PEDRO Now, signior, where's the count? did you see him?	**DON PEDRO** Now, Sir, where's Claudio? Have you seen him?
BENEDICK Troth, my lord, I have played the part of Lady Fame. I found him here as melancholy as a lodge in a warren: I told him, and I think I told him true, that your grace had got the good will of this young lady; and I offered him my company to a willow-tree, either to make him a garland, as being forsaken, or to bind him up a rod, as being worthy to be whipped.	**BENEDICK** Indeed I have, my lord, and I have played the part of the gossip. I found him here looking all sad and lonely, so I told him, and I think I told him the truth, that you had won Hero's affections. So I offered to accompany him to a willow-tree where he could either make himself a garland to show he's been rejected or a bundle of sticks to be whipped with.
DON PEDRO To be whipped! What's his fault?	**DON PEDRO** To be whipped! What was his crime?
BENEDICK The flat transgression of a schoolboy, who, being overjoyed with finding a birds' nest, shows it his companion, and he steals it.	**BENEDICK** The crime of a schoolboy, who's so excited about finding a birds' nest that he shows it his friend, and the friend then steals it.
DON PEDRO Wilt thou make a trust a transgression? The transgression is in the stealer.	**DON PEDRO** Why are calling trusting your friend a crime? The criminal is the one who stole the nest.
BENEDICK Yet it had not been amiss the rod had been made, and the garland too; for the garland he might have worn himself, and the rod he might have bestowed on you, who, as I take it, have stolen his birds' nest.	**BENEDICK** And yet it wouldn't have been a bad idea to make the rod and garland; it would still be appropriate to wear the garland, and the rod he might have used on you, who, I believe, has stolen his birds' nest.

DON PEDRO I will but teach them to sing, and restore them to the owner.	**DON PEDRO** My intention is only to teach the baby birds to sing, then I'll return the nest to its rightful owner
BENEDICK If their singing answer your saying, by my faith, you say honestly.	**BENEDICK** If the song they sing is the one you say it is, that Hero is keen on Claudio, then we'll know you're telling the truth.
DON PEDRO The Lady Beatrice hath a quarrel to you: the gentleman that danced with her told her she is much wronged by you.	**DON PEDRO** Beatrice is angry with you: the gentleman she danced with her told her you've done her wrong.
BENEDICK O, she misused me past the endurance of a block! an oak but with one green leaf on it would have answered her; my very visor began to assume life and scold with her. She told me, not thinking I had been myself, that I was the prince's jester, that I was duller than a great thaw; huddling jest upon jest with such impossible conveyance upon me that I stood like a man at a mark, with a whole army shooting at me. She speaks poniards, and every word stabs: if her breath were as terrible as her terminations, there were no living near her; she would infect to the north star. I would not marry her, though she were endowed with all that Adam bad left him before he transgressed: she would have made Hercules have turned spit, yea, and have cleft his club to make the fire too. Come, talk not of her: you shall find her the infernal Ate in good apparel. I would to God some scholar would conjure her; for certainly, while she is here, a man may live as quiet in hell as in a sanctuary; and people sin upon purpose, because they would go thither; so, indeed, all disquiet, horror and perturbation follows her.	**BENEDICK** Not even block of wood could put up with the way she abused me! An oak tree with only the smallest sign of life would have fought back; even my mask seemed about to come to life and tell her what's what. She told me, not realising it was *me* she was talking to, that I was the Prince's court jester, that I was more boring than a wet weekend; she piled joke on joke at my expense so quickly that it was like it was like having a whole army shooting at me. She speaks daggers, and every word stabs: if her breath were as terrible as her words, nothing could survive between here and the north star. I wouldn't marry her, even if she had inherited the whole of paradise. If she were married to Hercules, she'd have made him do the cooking, and even chop up his club for firewood. Please don't talk about her: she is Ate, the goddess of mischief and ruin disguised in pretty clothes. I would to God some learned man would magic her away, because as long as she's about there is no peace -people sin deliberately to go to hell because it's more peaceful that being where she is. Chaos, dismay and trouble follow where she goes.
DON PEDRO Look, here she comes.	**DON PEDRO** Look, here she comes.
Enter CLAUDIO, BEATRICE, HERO, and LEONATO	*CLAUDIO, BEATRICE, HERO, and LEONATO enter*
BENEDICK Will your grace command me any service to the world's end? I will go on the slightest errand now to the Antipodes that you can devise to send me on; I will fetch you a tooth-picker now from the furthest inch of Asia, bring you the length of Prester John's foot, fetch you a hair off the great Cham's beard, do you any embassage to the Pigmies,	**BENEDICK** Will your grace please send me on a mission to the far ends on the earth? I will go to the opposite side of the world on the most trivial errand you can think of; I will fetch you a toothpick from the far end of Asia, find out Prester John's shoe size, fetch you a hair from the Mongol Emperor's beard, deliver a message to the Pygmies - anything, rather than

rather than hold three words' conference with this harpy. You have no employment for me?	exchange three words with this awful woman. Is there no job you have for me?
DON PEDRO None, but to desire your good company.	**DON PEDRO** None, except being good company.
BENEDICK O God, sir, here's a dish I love not: I cannot endure my Lady Tongue.	**BENEDICK** O God, sir, here comes a dish I don't like: I can't stand tongue!
Exit	*He exits*
DON PEDRO Come, lady, come; you have lost the heart of Signior Benedick.	**DON PEDRO** (*to* BEATRICE) Come now, lady; you seem to have lost Sir Benedick's heart.
BEATRICE Indeed, my lord, he lent it me awhile; and I gave him use for it, a double heart for his single one: marry, once before he won it of me with false dice, therefore your grace may well say I have lost it.	**BEATRICE** It's true, my lord - he lent it to me for a while; and I returned it with interest - two for the price of one. Really he won it from me previously by trickery, so you may well say I have lost it.
DON PEDRO You have put him down, lady, you have put him down.	**DON PEDRO** You've humiliated him lady, put him down.
BEATRICE So I would not he should do me, my lord, lest I should prove the mother of fools. I have brought Count Claudio, whom you sent me to seek.	**BEATRICE** Well I hope he never puts me down on a bed, my lord, or I would give birth to fools. I brought Count Claudio, who you sent me to look for.
DON PEDRO Why, how now, count! wherefore are you sad?	**DON PEDRO** What's the trouble, Count! Why are you so sad?
CLAUDIO Not sad, my lord.	**CLAUDIO** I'm not sad, my lord.
DON PEDRO How then? sick?	**DON PEDRO** What then? Sick?
CLAUDIO Neither, my lord.	**CLAUDIO** Not sick either, my lord.
BEATRICE The count is neither sad, nor sick, nor merry, nor well; but civil count, civil as an orange, and something of that jealous complexion.	**BEATRICE** The Count is neither sad nor sick nor happy nor well - he's just civil - or is it 'Seville' like the bitter marmalade orange, for he has something of the bitter look of jealousy about him.
DON PEDRO I' faith, lady, I think your blazon to be true; though, I'll be sworn, if he be so, his conceit is false. Here, Claudio, I have wooed in thy name, and fair Hero is won: I have broke with her father, and his good will obtained: name the day of marriage, and God give thee joy!	**DON PEDRO** In truth, lady, I think your description is correct, though I swear that if it is the case, he's mistaken. Here, Claudio, I have wooed Hero for you, and won her hand in marriage for you. I have discussed it with her father, and he gives his consent. Just name the day and God give you joy!

LEONATO Count, take of me my daughter, and with her my fortunes: his grace hath made the match, and all grace say Amen to it.	**LEONATO** Count, take my daughter, and with her my fortunes. His grace the Prince has made the match, and may gracious God bless it.
BEATRICE Speak, count, 'tis your cue.	**BEATRICE** Speak, Claudio - that's your cue.
CLAUDIO Silence is the perfectest herald of joy: I were but little happy, if I could say how much. Lady, as you are mine, I am yours: I give away myself for you and dote upon the exchange.	**CLAUDIO** My silence shows just how happy I am; if I were able to say how happy I was, it would mean I was only a little happy. Lady you are mine and I am yours. I give myself to you as you give yourself to me, and I'm overjoyed by the exchange.
BEATRICE Speak, cousin; or, if you cannot, stop his mouth with a kiss, and let not him speak neither.	**BEATRICE** Say something, cousin; or, if you can't then stop his mouth up with a kiss so he can't speak either.
DON PEDRO In faith, lady, you have a merry heart.	**DON PEDRO** Truly, lady, you have a merry heart.
BEATRICE Yea, my lord; I thank it, poor fool, it keeps on the windy side of care. My cousin tells him in his ear that he is in her heart.	**BEATRICE** Yes, my lord. I thank it - the poor fool - that it steers clear of seriousness. Look - my cousin is whispering into Claudio's ear that he has a place in her heart.
CLAUDIO And so she doth, cousin.	**CLAUDIO** That is exactly right, cousin.
BEATRICE Good Lord, for alliance! Thus goes everyone to the world but I, and I am sunburnt; I may sit in a corner and cry heigh-ho for a husband!	**BEATRICE** Thank the Lord for marriage! So goes everyone out into the world except me, who is rough and sunburned. I'll just sit in a corner and tearfully quote that song 'heigh-ho for a husband'!
DON PEDRO Lady Beatrice, I will get you one.	**DON PEDRO** I will get you one, Lady Beatrice.
BEATRICE I would rather have one of your father's getting. Hath your grace ne'er a brother like you? Your father got excellent husbands, if a maid could come by them.	**BEATRICE** I'd rather your father produced one for me. Doesn't your grace have any brothers like you? Your father raised excellent husbands, if a girl could only catch one.
DON PEDRO Will you have me, lady?	**DON PEDRO** Will you take me, lady?
BEATRICE No, my lord, unless I might have another for working-days: your grace is too costly to wear every day. But, I beseech your grace, pardon me: I was born to speak all mirth and no matter.	**BEATRICE** No, my lord, unless I could have another husband for working days: you are too expensive for every day wear. But please forgive me, your grace: My nature is to joke rather than talk seriously.

DON PEDRO Your silence most offends me, and to be merry best becomes you; for, out of question, you were born in a merry hour.	**DON PEDRO** I'd be much more offended if you were silent - being merry is what suits you best. Without doubt you were born at a merry hour.
BEATRICE No, sure, my lord, my mother cried; but then there was a star danced, and under that was I born. Cousins, God give you joy!	**BEATRICE** Absolutely not, my lord: my mother cried while she was in labour. But then a star danced in the sky and that was when I was born. Cousins, I wish you joy!
LEONATO Niece, will you look to those things I told you of?	**LEONATO** Niece, will you deal with those things I told you about?
BEATRICE I cry you mercy, uncle. By your grace's pardon. *Exit*	**BEATRICE** Oh yes! Sorry, uncle. Please excuse me, your grace. *She exits.*
DON PEDRO By my troth, a pleasant-spirited lady.	**DON PEDRO** She's certainly a high-spirited lady.
LEONATO There's little of the melancholy element in her, my lord: she is never sad but when she sleeps, and not ever sad then; for I have heard my daughter say, she hath often dreamed of unhappiness and waked herself with laughing.	**LEONATO** There's very little gloominess in her, my lord. She's never sad except when she's asleep, and actually not even then; Hero told me that Beatrice often had unhappy dreams but woke up laughing.
DON PEDRO She cannot endure to hear tell of a husband.	**DON PEDRO** She can't stand talk about getting a husband.
LEONATO O, by no means: she mocks all her wooers out of suit.	**LEONATO** Absolutely not: she mocks all her suitors to the point where they give up.
DON PEDRO She were an excellent wife for Benedick.	**DON PEDRO** She'd make a perfect wife for Benedick.
LEONATO O Lord, my lord, if they were but a week married, they would talk themselves mad.	**LEONATO** Goodness no, my lord - they'd drive each other mad within a week.
DON PEDRO County Claudio, when mean you to go to church?	**DON PEDRO** Count Claudio, when do you intend to get married?
CLAUDIO To-morrow, my lord: time goes on crutches till love have all his rites.	**CLAUDIO** Tomorrow, my lord. Time will move as slowly as man on crutches until love gets its ceremony.
LEONATO Not till Monday, my dear son, which is hence a just seven-night; and a time too brief, too, to have all things answer my mind.	**LEONATO** Wait until next Monday, my dear son: it's only a week away, and even that is too short a time to make the plans I want.
DON PEDRO Come, you shake the head at so long a breathing: but, I warrant thee, Claudio, the time shall not go	**DON PEDRO** Come, Claudio you shake your head at having to wait so long but, the time will go quickly, I promise.

dully by us. I will in the interim undertake one of Hercules' labours; which is, to bring Signior Benedick and the Lady Beatrice into a mountain of affection the one with the other. I would fain have it a match, and I doubt not but to fashion it, if you three will but minister such assistance as I shall give you direction.	Meanwhile, like Hercules, I will undertake a seemingly impossible task, that of making Benedick and Beatrice fall in love with each other. I intend to see them together, and I'm sure that with help from all of you, I shall achieve it.
LEONATO My lord, I am for you, though it cost me ten nights' watchings.	**LEONATO** My lord, I will help you, even if it means staying up ten nights in a row.
CLAUDIO And I, my lord.	**CLAUDIO** Me too, my lord.
DON PEDRO And you too, gentle Hero?	**DON PEDRO** And you, Hero, my dear?
HERO I will do any modest office, my lord, to help my cousin to a good husband.	**HERO** I will do anything that's not immoral, my lord, to help my cousin get a good husband.
DON PEDRO And Benedick is not the unhopefullest husband that I know. Thus far can I praise him; he is of a noble strain, of approved valour and confirmed honesty. I will teach you how to humour your cousin, that she shall fall in love with Benedick; and I, with your two helps, will so practise on Benedick that, in despite of his quick wit and his queasy stomach, he shall fall in love with Beatrice. If we can do this, Cupid is no longer an archer: his glory shall be ours, for we are the only love-gods. Go in with me, and I will tell you my drift.	**DON PEDRO** And Benedick is not the most hopeless husband that I can think of. I'll say this for him: he is of good birth, he's demonstrated his bravery and he is honest. I'll teach you how to influence your cousin, to fall in love with Benedick. Meanwhile we men will work on Benedick so well that despite his cleverness and distaste for her, he will fall in love with Beatrice. If we manage this, we'll put Cupid out of a job; we'll be the love-gods! Come inside with me, and I will tell you my plan.
Exeunt	*They all exit*

Analysis of Act 2 Scene 1

To make sense of this scene it is best to think of a series of snap-shots, showing what's happening at the party.

Summary:
The scene opens with gossipy chatter: from mocking Don John's sullen [hostile/ surly] behaviour the conversation moves to Benedick and so to husbands and Beatrice's determination not to marry. Both Leonato and Antonio remind Hero to remember to do what they told her to do with regard to Don Pedro, but Beatrice warns her about marriage and tells her to make sure she pleases herself too.

When the guests enter, Don Pedro singles Hero out immediately and because she's been warned to expect wooing, Hero's responses are quite flirty. Various dancers meet and guess who is behind the mask. They also say things they might not normally say to each other. Borachio chats up Margaret; Antonio and Ursula flirt; Beatrice uses the opportunity to mock Benedick; Don John uses the anonymity of the mask to pretend he thinks Claudio is Benedick and warns him that Don Pedro is actually going to marry Hero himself. Claudio immediately believes that his friend has double crossed him and is bitter.

Benedick, who didn't hear Don Pedro promise to woo Hero on Claudio's behalf [Act1 scene1], probably also believes that Don Pedro loves Hero, but he finds it amusing and expects Claudio to be able to laugh it off when he teases him. Claudio is upsets and leaves. Benedick thinks about what Beatrice said about him and vows revenge. When Don Pedro arrives he tells him that Claudio is upset, so Don Pedro explains the true situation and the audience hears that Hero will marry Claudio. Then he tells Benedick that Beatrice has told him that one of her dance partners [they both know it is Benedick] told her that Benedick has been slandering her. This infuriates Benedick, who blurts out how hurt he has been by the insulting things she said about him and when she appears he begs to be sent on an errand to get as far away from her as possible. He leaves, saying he can't stand her.

Don Pedro tells Beatrice she's gone too far and lost Benedick's heart; she confesses that they were once close, but both cheated on each other, hence the mistrust and 'war' between them. Neither wants the other to get the upper hand. She tries to turn it into a joke by suggesting if she let Benedick get on top of her, she'd have babies as stupid as he is.

Beatrice then says she's brought Claudio as asked and hints at why he is so miserable, which gives Don Pedro the opportunity of breaking the good news to Claudio: everything is arranged, he just needs to name the wedding day. [Notice that he doesn't say a word!]

Beatrice then bemoans the fact that everyone is getting married except her. However, when Don Pedro offers to marry her she says he's too good for her ['costly']. As soon as she leaves on an errand Leonato reminds her of, Don Pedro says she would make an excellent wife for Benedick. He asks the others to help him bring Beatrice and Benedick together and they agree to do so.

Genre:
Another characteristic of comedy is the tricks that can be played when people wear masks. We call this a **convention** [pact/arrangement], because we all agree – as part of the 'game' of comedy- to believe in the disguising power of masks, though as Ursula shows when talking to Antonio, it is actually quite easy to recognise people from their mannerisms, voice etc. Because of this, people are able to say things to each other they couldn't normally say. Notice how Benedick can't defend himself against Beatrice's attack without giving away the fact that he is Benedick - whom he

pretends not to know- which he can't do because he has already slandered her as if he didn't know he was talking to her. Don John, recognising Claudio, uses the mask to his own advantage: he pretends he thinks Claudio is Benedick and so suggests he could be a good friend to Claudio by letting him know that Don Pedro has double-crossed him and is actually going to marry Hero himself, that very night!

Form:
It is important to remember that the text you are reading is a play: this is the script, but it needs actors to bring it to life and they do that in so many different ways that every production of the play has its own insights and interpretations. In one, Benedick speaks in a funny voice to ensure he isn't recognised, in another Beatrice and Benedick are middle aged, suggesting their on/off affair has been going on for years. The actors can suggest a more intimate relationship exists between Barachio and Margaret, for example, based on claims he makes later in the play.

So Benedick's response to Claudio's sulks about Don Pedro 'stealing' Hero could also be played two ways. If we assume he knows nothing of the plan to woo Hero on Claudio's behalf, he might think the Prince, Don Pedro, has beaten Claudio to it and mean it when he suggests the willow garland of abandoned lovers is what Claudio needs. On the other hand, it is likely that he has heard the plan, sees Claudio moping and can't believe he really thinks Don Pedro would cheat on him, so he is sarcastic when he suggests ways in which to wear the willow.

Similarly, some productions suggest Don Pedro might be a little in love with Beatrice when he asks her to marry him, others show it as a way of testing her – is she hinting, or is she regretting her determination never to marry?

One of the reasons Shakespeare has remained fresh and interesting for over 400 years is because there is plenty of scope [opportunity] for interpretation. When you write about the text, remember that you can also mention alternative interpretations, so if you can, watch lots of different productions of the play, or at least clips of them.

Structure:
This scene is made up of lots of min-scenes, 'snap-shots' of what is happening at the party, little 'episodes', so we call the structure of this scene **episodic**. Each change of focus is like a puzzle piece of the bigger picture which builds on information we as the audience remember from Act 1 and prepares the way for the action of the rest of the play.

The scene begins with Beatrice scorning marriage in as much detail as Benedick has done in Act1, immediately emphasising the connection between them that each is energetically denying. We see more of the on-going 'merry war' between Beatrice and Benedick, Hero is wooed and won for Claudio, Don John begins the mischief he began to plot in Act1 by suggesting he has been betrayed. Slipped in so that it doesn't stand out too much is a 'seed' sown that will bear fruit later in the play: Borachio's relationship with Margaret.

The cliff-hanger of the scene is Don Pedro's announcement that he plans to get Beatrice and Benedick to marry each other.

Themes:

- Marriage

When Beatrice turns down Don Pedro's proposal, it is clear to him that she must be in love –as he has suspected – with Benedick, because he would be a good catch for her. She seems not to have parents, though she is financially secure enough not to be treated like a servant in her uncle's home

[NB She is NOT Antonio's daughter, though he is Hero's uncle and Leonato is her uncle]. She calls him 'too costly' because she knows he is of a higher social status and also that she would not be able to play the role of Princess: she's too opinionated. While men have more freedom –despite Benedick's description of marriage being to: 'thrust thy neck into a yoke, wear the print of it and sigh away Sundays'- women are expected to be obedient to fathers and husbands, as Hero has already been ordered to be by her father and her uncle at the start of the scene. Beatrice tells her to please herself, an attitude unsuited to the role of Don Pedro's wife.

- Appearance vs. reality

The masks in this scene emphasise that things aren't necessarily as they appear. They allow deceptions like Don John's lie to Claudio and the slanders Beatrice and Benedick report to hurt each other. Don Perdo looks as if he is chatting Hero up, but in reality he is sticking to his deal with Claudio and winning her on his behalf. Don John appears to be giving Claudio helpful advice via his friend Benedick, but in reality he is trying to hurt Claudio and bring his brother into disrepute [discredit/ dishonour].

Characters:

- Beatrice and Benedick

We see how similar they are, beginning with Beatrice's tirade against marriage, which is so similar to Benedick's in Act1 scene1. Just as Benedick unwittingly revealed that he thinks Beatrice is more beautiful than Hero, Beatrice, talking about Don John suggests that a mix between him and Benedick would make the ideal husband. The fact that they can both still hurt each other proves that they care what the other thinks of them. With their past relationship revealed and the evidence that Beartice is not looking to marry anyone else – not even a catch like Don Pedro – the way is clear to plot their union; after all, Don Pedro wants to see Benedick 'look pale with love'.

- Claudio

In this scene we see wonder-boy Claudio is not the great man he seems. He sulks like a child when he thinks Don Pedro is wooing Hero for himself, instead of trying to interrupt or call him out. Worse – you might excuse him on the grounds that Don Pedro is his leader, superior in rank, so he couldn't contradict his claim on Hero- is that he believes a 'known villain', Don John, over his close friend, Don Pedro, a man of honour. This gullible doubt in the people he holds dear when his own honour is threatened is a characteristic that will be exploited by Don John again in the play.

When his fear is proved wrong, he doesn't apologise for thinking so badly of his friend, nor does he say how relieved and delighted he is that Hero will have him – it takes Beatrice to urge his to say something before he says he's too happy to say anything. Watch this space: having to apologise and admit his mistakes is a lesson he has to learn in this play.

Act 2 Scene 2

ORIGINAL TEXT	MODERN TRANSLATION
The same.	**The same place.**
Enter DON JOHN and BORACHIO	*DON JOHN and BORACHIO enter*
DON JOHN It is so; the Count Claudio shall marry the daughter of Leonato.	**DON JOHN** So it's all arranged: Count Claudio will marry the Leonato's daughter.
BORACHIO Yea, my lord; but I can cross it.	**BORACHIO** Yes, my lord; but I can spoil it.
DON JOHN Any bar, any cross, any impediment will be medicinable to me: I am sick in displeasure to him, and whatsoever comes athwart his affection ranges evenly with mine. How canst thou cross this marriage?	**DON JOHN** Any spanner you can throw in the works would be like medicine to me. I dislike him so much it makes me feel ill, so anything that spoils things for him makes me feel better. What can you do to wreck the marriage ?
BORACHIO Not honestly, my lord; but so covertly that no dishonesty shall appear in me.	**BORACHIO** It'll mean telling a few lies, my lord, but secretly, so that no-one suspects me.
DON JOHN Show me briefly how.	**DON JOHN** Give me a quick idea how.
BORACHIO I think I told your lordship a year since, how much I am in the favour of Margaret, the waiting gentlewoman to Hero.	**BORACHIO** About a year ago, I think, I told your lordship how Margaret, Hero's servant woman, like me.
DON JOHN I remember.	**DON JOHN** Yes,I remember.
BORACHIO I can, at any unseasonable instant of the night, appoint her to look out at her lady's chamber window.	**BORACHIO** I can get her to look out of her Hero's bedroom window at some indecent hour of the night.
DON JOHN What life is in that, to be the death of this marriage?	**DON JOHN** How will that put an end to the marriage?
BORACHIO The poison of that lies in you to temper. Go you to the prince your brother; spare not to tell him that he hath wronged his honour in marrying the renowned Claudio--whose estimation do you mightily hold up--to a contaminated stale, such a one as Hero.	**BORACHIO** That's where you poison things. Go to your brother, the Prince, and tell him it will reflect badly on him to allow Claudio-- whom you admire greatly -- to marry a slut like Hero.
DON JOHN What proof shall I make of that?	**DON JOHN** What evidence shall I give him?

BORACHIO Proof enough to misuse the prince, to vex Claudio, to undo Hero and kill Leonato. Look you for any other issue?	**BORACHIO** Evidence enough to deceive the prince, anger Claudio, ruin Hero and kill Leonato. Will that be enough for you?
DON JOHN Only to despite them, I will endeavour any thing.	**DON JOHN** I'll do what it takes to make it happen.
BORACHIO Go, then; find me a meet hour to draw Don Pedro and the Count Claudio alone: tell them that you know that Hero loves me; intend a kind of zeal both to the prince and Claudio, as,--in love of your brother's honour, who hath made this match, and his friend's reputation, who is thus like to be cozened with the semblance of a maid,--that you have discovered thus. They will scarcely believe this without trial: offer them instances; which shall bear no less likelihood than to see me at her chamber-window, hear me call Margaret Hero, hear Margaret term me Claudio; and bring them to see this the very night before the intended wedding,--for in the meantime I will so fashion the matter that Hero shall be absent,--and there shall appear such seeming truth of Hero's disloyalty that jealousy shall be called assurance and all the preparation overthrown.	**BORACHIO** OK then - find a time to speak Don Pedro and Claudio alone. Tell them that you have discovered that Hero loves me; make out you're very concerned about damage to the good name of both the Prince, who set the wedding up and Claudio, who stands to be fooled into thinking he's marrying a virgin. Of course they'll want proof. Tell them you've seen me at her window, and then, the night before the wedding, bring them to the window themselves, I'll make sure Hero's away and then set it up so they see me at the window with Margaret, calling each other 'Hero' and 'Claudio'; It will be such convincing proof of Hero's unfaithfulness that Claudio's jealousy will get the better of him and the wedding will be called off.. Meanwhile, I'll arrange that Hero will be absent, so that her disloyalty will appear true and Claudio's jealousy will ensure he's convinced - and all the wedding preparations will be wasted.
DON JOHN Grow this to what adverse issue it can, I will put it in practise. Be cunning in the working this, and thy fee is a thousand ducats.	**DON JOHN** Make this as damaging as you can and I'll do it. If you're wily enough to pull it off, I'll reward you with a thousand gold coins.
BORACHIO Be you constant in the accusation, and my cunning shall not shame me.	**BORACHIO** If you can make the accusation convincing, my scheming will not let me down.
DON JOHN I will presently go learn their day of marriage. *Exeunt*	**DON JOHN** I'll go right away to find out what day the wedding is. *They exit*

Analysis of Act 2 Scene 2

Having almost succeeded in causing a rift between Claudio and Don Pedro, the bad boys of the play are ready to try again.

Summary:
Unwittingly, Margaret, Hero's companion, is to be the 'enemy within', the traitor. Borachio is so sure that she will do as he asks - allow herself to be called Hero, arrange for the real Hero to sleep elsewhere and even to call him Claudio – that he is able to plot the perfect revenge: preventing Claudio and Hero's marriage.

Don John has to pretend to like both his brother, Don Pedro, and Claudio so much that he is concerned about their honour when Claudio marries – with Don Pedro's approval –someone little better than a common prostitute, which, he'll claim, Hero is. Apart from ruining the wedding, the shame and shock of it could kill Leonato.

The plan is to use Claudio's jealous nature against him: Borachio is confident that he'll immediately believe what he fears – that Hero is indeed unfaithful. The reality will be that Borachio will be indulging in a bit of role play with Margaret at Hero's bedroom window, calling her Hero and behaving like lovers.

Genre:
Mistaken identity is yet another characteristic of comedy that we're familiar with from TV sitcoms. Here it is purposefully contrived [manufactured] to cause maximum damage. Shakespearian comedy is not 'laugh a minute' comedy; although it does have some lines that could raise a laugh, the main idea behind dramatic comedy is the celebration of life, things end happily, people get married [to have children and so perpetuate (carry on) life]rather than things being 'comic'.

Context:
In the days before genetic testing was possible, a man couldn't always be sure a child was his, unless his partner was a virgin who remained faithful to him. No man wanted his efforts in building both reputation and wealth to be wasted on some other man's child, so being a virtuous [moral/ honest] virgin was vital in a wife. Remember how Benedick went on about being 'cuckolded' [deceived/ cheated] in Act1 scene1? His fear of being taken for a fool by a woman is what keeps him a bachelor. So Claudio, who values his honour and good name, would definitely not want to marry someone who seemed to be sleeping around.

Margaret, on the other hand, is of a lower social class: not quite a servant, but without money to attract a suitor [remember how even Count Claudio wanted to be sure his lovely Hero would inherit Leonato's fortune before saying how much he longed to marry her]. Probably her father had a position of trust in Leonato's employ and the girls had grown up together and likely she'd be married off to a widower of similar status for a comfortable, but not wealthy, life once she'd past into middle age, maybe having been a nanny to Hero's children... She would be up for a bit of excitement and happy to try and lure someone like Borachio – of similar or slightly higher social standing into a love relationship; a risk worth taking for the possible payoff. It is unlikely that she would actually sleep with him; they would flirt and maybe kiss: wooing would seem very innocent to today's audiences, so many modern productions hint at far more than Shakespeare's audience would have allowed possible.

Themes:

- Marriage

To someone like Claudio, marriage was not just a physical union – husband and wife became one in the sight of God and their children needed good blood from both parents. He would be eternally shamed by a wife that was not completely honorable. His friends would not be able to associate with him if he married someone 'impure', a sinner. Don Pedro, who arranged it all would likewise be brought into disrepute by Hero's supposed immorality. There might even be a suspicion that Leonato was taking them for a ride, trying to palm his 'spoilt goods' off on them by being such a good host, so willing to have Claudio as a son-in-law.

- Appearance vs. reality

This scene goes further than the last – the masks are not needed anymore because Claudio has shown how ready he is to fall for Don John's tricks: his eyes will believe what is suggested to him.

Characters:

- Don John

Some of Shakespeare's villains are hypocrites [frauds], but some, like Don John [and Iago in *Othello*] are quite open about their villainy. He is open about how much he wants to hurt both Claudio and his brother, Don Pedro and is prepared to reward Borachio generously if the plan works. However, you could argue that he relies too heavily on the advice of others: they think up the plots and warn him about keeping up appearances so that he isn't immediately suspected... maybe he's not such an accomplished villain after all: watch this space.

Act 2 Scene 3

ORIGINAL TEXT	MODERN TRANSLATION
LEONATO'S orchard.	**LEONATO'S orchard.**
Enter BENEDICK	*BENEDICK enters*
BENEDICK Boy!	**BENEDICK** Boy!
Enter Boy	*Boy enters*
Boy Signior?	**Boy** Yes, Sir?
BENEDICK In my chamber-window lies a book: bring it hither to me in the orchard.	**BENEDICK** There's a book on the window-sill of my bedroom. Bring it to me here in the orchard.
Boy I am here already, sir.	**Boy** I am already here, sir.
BENEDICK I know that; but I would have thee hence, and here again.	**BENEDICK** I know that you are here, but I would like you to go there and then come back here.
Exit Boy	*The boy exits*
I do much wonder that one man, seeing how much another man is a fool when he dedicates his behaviors to love, will, after he hath laughed at such shallow follies in others, become the argument of his own scorn by falling in love: and such a man is Claudio. I have known when there was no music with him but the drum and the fife; and now had he rather hear the tabour and the pipe: I have known when he would have walked ten mile a-foot to see a good armour; and now will he lie ten nights awake, carving the fashion of a new doublet. He was wont to speak plain and to the purpose, like an honest man and a soldier; and now is he turned orthography; his words are a very fantastical banquet, just so many strange dishes. May I be so converted and see with these eyes? I cannot tell; I think not: I will not be sworn, but love may transform me to an oyster; but I'll take my oath on it, till he have made an oyster of me, he shall never make me such a fool. One woman is fair, yet I am well; another is wise, yet I am well; another virtuous, yet I am well; but till all graces be in one woman, one woman shall not come in my grace. Rich she shall be, that's certain; wise, or I'll none; virtuous, or I'll never cheapen her; fair, or I'll never look on her; mild, or come not near me;	It amazes me that anybody, after seeing what a fool love turns another man into, and laughing at his stupidity, can still turn into the object of his own scorn by falling in love himself. But Claudio is such a man. I knew him when the only music he wanted to hear was the military drum and fife; and now he's only interested in dance music. I remember when he would have walked ten miles to see a good suit of armour, but now he'll lie awake for ten nights designing a new jacket for himself. He used to speak plainly and to the point, like an honest man and a soldier; and now he uses flowery language - his words are like a fantasy banquet full of strange dishes. Could that happen to me? I can't be sure, but I don't think so. I can't swear that love won't turn me into a lump of jelly like an oyster, but unless it does, it won't make me into a fool. One woman is beautiful, but I can handle it. Another might be smart: no problem; another good and moral - I can handle that too. It would take all three of those qualities being combined in one woman to win me over. She's have to be rich, too; and smart, or she's a non-starter,; virtuous, or I won't even court her;beautiful, or I won't look twice at her; mild-mannered , or she won't get near me; noble of birth

noble, or not I for an angel; of good discourse, an excellent musician, and her hair shall be of what colour it please God. Ha! the prince and Monsieur Love! I will hide me in the arbour. *Withdraws*	and character, or she's not for me, interesting to talk to, an excellent musician - and her hair should be .. well, whatever colour God chooses. Aha! It's the Prince and Mister Lover! I'll hide in the bushes. *He hides*
Enter DON PEDRO, CLAUDIO, and LEONATO	*DON PEDRO, CLAUDIO, and LEONATO enter.*
DON PEDRO Come, shall we hear this music?	**DON PEDRO** Come, shall we listen to some music?
CLAUDIO Yea, my good lord. How still the evening is, As hush'd on purpose to grace harmony!	**CLAUDIO** Yes, my lord. The evening is so still, as if on purpose to help the music sound its best.
DON PEDRO See you where Benedick hath hid himself?	**DON PEDRO** Did you see where Benedick is hiding?
CLAUDIO O, very well, my lord: the music ended, We'll fit the kid-fox with a pennyworth.	**CLAUDIO** I saw very well, my lord: when the music is over, we'll give the crafty young fox something more than he's bargained for.
Enter BALTHASAR with Music	*BALTHASAR enters with music.*
DON PEDRO Come, Balthasar, we'll hear that song again.	**DON PEDRO** Come, Balthasar, let's hear that song again.
BALTHASAR O, good my lord, tax not so bad a voice To slander music any more than once.	**BALTHASAR** O, good my lord, don't insult the music with my poor voice more than once
DON PEDRO It is the witness still of excellency To put a strange face on his own perfection. I pray thee, sing, and let me woo no more.	**DON PEDRO** You can tell an artist is excellent when he is modest about how good he is. Please sing, and don't make me have to woo you anymore!
BALTHASAR Because you talk of wooing, I will sing; Since many a wooer doth commence his suit To her he thinks not worthy, yet he wooes, Yet will he swear he loves.	**BALTHASAR** Since you put it in terms of wooing, I will sing, because many wooers swear they love the lady though they don't actually think she's worthy of them.
DON PEDRO Now, pray thee, come; Or, if thou wilt hold longer argument, Do it in notes.	**DON PEDRO** Come on now, please sing - or if you want to go on arguing, at least set it to music!
BALTHASAR Note this before my notes; There's not a note of mine that's worth the noting.	**BALTHASAR** Just note before I sing a note: There's not a note of mine that's worth noting.
DON PEDRO Why, these are very crotchets that he speaks; Note, notes, forsooth, and nothing.	**DON PEDRO** What strange notions he has! Note or notes, indeed! Was it noting or nothing?

Air	*Music*
BENEDICK Now, divine air! now is his soul ravished! Is it not strange that sheeps' guts should hale souls out of men's bodies? Well, a horn for my money, when all's done.	**BENEDICK** That music like music of the gods, it captivates the soul! It's so strange that strings made out of sheep-gut should have the power to call men's souls out of their bodies? But I'd rather listen to a horn, when all's said and done.
The Song	*The Song*
BALTHASAR Sigh no more, ladies, sigh no more, Men were deceivers ever, One foot in sea and one on shore, To one thing constant never: Then sigh not so, but let them go, And be you blithe and bonny, Converting all your sounds of woe Into Hey nonny, nonny. Sing no more ditties, sing no moe, Of dumps so dull and heavy; The fraud of men was ever so, Since summer first was leafy: Then sigh not so, but let them go, And be you blithe and bonny, Converting all your sounds of woe Into Hey nonny, nonny.	**BALTHASAR** (*sings*) Cry no more, ladies, cry no more, Men were always deceivers, One foot in the sea and one on the shore, Never settling on either: So don't cry so, just let them go, And you be carefree and bonny, Changing all your sounds of woe Into 'Hey nonny, nonny.' Sing no more rhymes, sing no more, Sad songs so full of grief Men have always practised fraud , Since Summer was the season of leaf: So don't cry so, just let them go, And you be carefree and bonny, Changing all your sounds of woe Into 'Hey nonny, nonny.'
DON PEDRO By my troth, a good song.	**DON PEDRO** That's a good song.
BALTHASAR And an ill singer, my lord.	**BALTHASAR** And a poor singer, my lord.
DON PEDRO Ha, no, no, faith; thou singest well enough for a shift.	**DON PEDRO** No - really! You sing better than anyone else here.
BENEDICK An he had been a dog that should have howled thus, they would have hanged him: and I pray God his bad voice bode no mischief. I had as lief have heard the night-raven, come what plague could have come after it.	**BENEDICK** (*to himself*) If it had been a dog howling like that they'd have hanged it! I hope and pray that his terrible voice doesn't mean trouble is coming, like a raven in the night is an omen of plague.
DON PEDRO Yea, marry, dost thou hear, Balthasar? I pray thee, get us some excellent music; for to-morrow night we would have it at the Lady Hero's chamber-window.	**DON PEDRO** Do you hear, Balthasar? Please, get us some excellent music: tomorrow night we want to serenade Lady Hero at her bedroom window.
BALTHASAR The best I can, my lord.	**BALTHASAR** I will get the best I can, my lord.
DON PEDRO Do so: farewell.	**DON PEDRO** Please do. Farewell.

Exit BALTHASAR	*BALTHASAR exits.*
Come hither, Leonato. What was it you told me of to-day, that your niece Beatrice was in love with Signior Benedick?	Come here, Leonato. What was it you told me to-day? That your niece Beatrice was in love with Sir Benedick?
CLAUDIO O, ay: stalk on. stalk on; the fowl sits. I did never think that lady would have loved any man.	**CLAUDIO** Oh yes! (*quietly to Leonato*) keep moving, we're close to where our prey is hiding! (*Out loud*) I never thought that woman would love any man.
LEONATO No, nor I neither; but most wonderful that she should so dote on Signior Benedick, whom she hath in all outward behaviors seemed ever to abhor.	**LEONATO** No, nor did I. But it's even more amazing that she should be in love with Signior Benedick, whom she acts like she hates
BENEDICK Is't possible? Sits the wind in that corner?	**BENEDICK** *(to himself)* Is that possible? Is that really the state of play?
LEONATO By my troth, my lord, I cannot tell what to think of it but that she loves him with an enraged affection: it is past the infinite of thought.	**LEONATO** Truly, my lord, I don't know what to make of it but that she's head over heels in love with him: it's beyond understanding.
DON PEDRO May be she doth but counterfeit.	**DON PEDRO** Could it be she's just pretending?
CLAUDIO Faith, like enough.	**CLAUDIO** Yes, that's probably it.
LEONATO O God, counterfeit! There was never counterfeit of passion came so near the life of passion as she discovers it.	**LEONATO** Pretending!! Nobody could fake such passion so convincingly!
DON PEDRO Why, what effects of passion shows she?	**DON PEDRO** How do you mean? What signs of passion does she show?
CLAUDIO Bait the hook well; this fish will bite.	**CLAUDIO** *(quietly to LEONATO)* Bait the hook well: this fish is ready to bite.
LEONATO What effects, my lord? She will sit you - you heard my daughter tell you how.	**LEONATO** What signs, my lord? It would amaze you - Claudio - my daughter told you about it, didn't she?
CLAUDIO She did, indeed.	**CLAUDIO** She did, indeed.
DON PEDRO How, how, pray you? You amaze me: I would have I thought her spirit had been invincible against all assaults of affection.	**DON PEDRO** How, how? Tell me! You amaze me! I would have thought she was immune to love!

LEONATO I would have sworn it had, my lord; especially against Benedick.	**LEONATO** I would have sworn she was, my lord; especially to loving Benedick.
BENEDICK I should think this a gull, but that the white-bearded fellow speaks it: knavery cannot, sure, hide himself in such reverence.	**BENEDICK** *(to himself)* I'd be sure this was a hoax if it wasn't coming from this old man: such a respectable fellow can't have such mischief in him.
CLAUDIO He hath ta'en the infection: hold it up.	**CLAUDIO** *(quietly, to Don Pedro)* He's swallowed our story: keep it up.
DON PEDRO Hath she made her affection known to Benedick?	**DON PEDRO** Has she told Benedick how she feels about him?
LEONATO No; and swears she never will: that's her torment.	**LEONATO** No - and she swears she never will. That's what's driving her crazy.
CLAUDIO 'Tis true, indeed; so your daughter says: 'Shall I,' says she, 'that have so oft encountered him with scorn, write to him that I love him?'	**CLAUDIO** It's true - that's what Hero says. Beatrice asks 'How can I, who has so often scorned him, now turn round and write to him that I love him?'
LEONATO This says she now when she is beginning to write to him; for she'll be up twenty times a night, and there will she sit in her smock till she have writ a sheet of paper: my daughter tells us all.	**LEONATO** That's what she says whenever she starts writing to him: but she'll get up twenty times a night and sit there in her nightie until she's written a page. My daughter told me everything.
CLAUDIO Now you talk of a sheet of paper, I remember a pretty jest your daughter told us of.	**CLAUDIO** Your mention of a sheet of paper, reminds me of that nice little joke your daughter told us
LEONATO O, when she had writ it and was reading it over, she found Benedick and Beatrice between the sheet?	**LEONATO** Oh yes - that when she'd written the letter, and was reading it over, she kept finding 'Benedick' and 'Beatrice' between the sheets?
CLAUDIO That.	**CLAUDIO** That's the one.
LEONATO O, she tore the letter into a thousand halfpence; railed at herself, that she should be so immodest to write to one that she knew would flout her; 'I measure him,' says she, 'by my own spirit; for I should flout him, if he writ to me; yea, though I love him, I should.'	**LEONATO** Then she tears the letter into a thousand tiny pieces and gets really cross with herself for being so open in writing like that to somebody she knew would mock her for it. 'It's what I'd do' she says, 'I know that I'd mock him if he wrote like that to me - even if I loved him, I would.'
CLAUDIO Then down upon her knees she falls, weeps, sobs, beats her heart, tears her hair, prays, curses; 'O sweet Benedick! God give me patience!'	**CLAUDIO** Then down she goes on her knees, weeps, sobs, beats her breast, tears her hair, prays and curses; 'Oh darling Benedick! God give me patience!'
LEONATO She doth indeed; my daughter says so: and the ecstasy hath so much overborne her that my	**LEONATO** That's exactly what Hero said she did: and Beatrice is sometimes so overcome with emotion that my daughter is worried she will harm herself. It's true.

daughter is sometime afeared she will do a desperate outrage to herself: it is very true.	
DON PEDRO It were good that Benedick knew of it by some other, if she will not discover it.	**DON PEDRO** Then somebody else must tell Benedick, if she won't.
CLAUDIO To what end? He would make but a sport of it and torment the poor lady worse.	**CLAUDIO** How would that help? He'd just make a game of it and torment the poor girl even more.
DON PEDRO An he should, it were an alms to hang him. She's an excellent sweet lady; and, out of all suspicion, she is virtuous.	**DON PEDRO** If he did that, it would be a charitable act to hang him! She's a really good, sweet young lady, and definitely still a virgin.
CLAUDIO And she is exceeding wise.	**CLAUDIO** And she's very clever.
DON PEDRO In every thing but in loving Benedick.	**DON PEDRO** Except for the fact that she loves Benedick.
LEONATO O, my lord, wisdom and blood combating in so tender a body, we have ten proofs to one that blood hath the victory. I am sorry for her, as I have just cause, being her uncle and her guardian.	**LEONATO** Oh, my lord - when reason fights with passion in so young a body, ten to one passion will win. I am sorry for her, as I should be, being both her uncle and her guardian.
DON PEDRO I would she had bestowed this dotage on me: I would have daffed all other respects and made her half myself. I pray you, tell Benedick of it, and hear what a' will say.	**DON PEDRO** I wish she felt that way about me: I'd just go for it and marry her. Please, just tell Benedick how she feels, and see what he says.
LEONATO Were it good, think you?	**LEONATO** Do you think that's a good idea?
CLAUDIO Hero thinks surely she will die; for she says she will die, if he love her not, and she will die, ere she make her love known, and she will die, if he woo her, rather than she will bate one breath of her accustomed crossness.	**CLAUDIO** Hero thinks Beatrice must surely die: she says she'll die if he doesn't love her, and she'll sooner die than tell him she loves him and if he tries to woo her she'll die if she has to hold back on her usual insults.
DON PEDRO She doth well: if she should make tender of her love, 'tis very possible he'll scorn it; for the man, as you know all, hath a contemptible spirit.	**DON PEDRO** She's actually right: if she simply offered him her love it's most likely he'd scorn it; we all know he has a contemptuous nature.
CLAUDIO He is a very proper man.	**CLAUDIO** He's a very good-looking man.
DON PEDRO He hath indeed a good outward happiness.	**DON PEDRO** He certainly has a fine outward appearance.
CLAUDIO Before God! and, in my mind, very wise.	**CLAUDIO** Absolutely - and very clever too, I think.

DON PEDRO He doth indeed show some sparks that are like wit.	**DON PEDRO** He does indeed show occasional sparks of something resembling wit.
CLAUDIO And I take him to be valiant.	**CLAUDIO** And, I believe he's brave, too.
DON PEDRO As Hector, I assure you: and in the managing of quarrels you may say he is wise; for either he avoids them with great discretion, or undertakes them with a most Christian-like fear.	**DON PEDRO** As brave as Hector, surely: and very clever at managing his fights, you might say he either discretely avoids them, or approaches them with the same fearful reverence as a Christian approaches God.
LEONATO If he do fear God, a' must necessarily keep peace: if he break the peace, he ought to enter into a quarrel with fear and trembling.	**LEONATO** If he does indeed fear God, it is his duty to keep the peace - and if he gets into a fight, then he should indeed go into it with fear and trembling.
DON PEDRO And so will he do; for the man doth fear God, howsoever it seems not in him by some large jests he will make. Well I am sorry for your niece. Shall we go seek Benedick, and tell him of her love?	**DON PEDRO** And so he does, for he is a God-fearing man, however much his coarse jokes make him seem otherwise. I am very sorry for your niece. Shall we go and find Benedick, and tell him she loves him?
CLAUDIO Never tell him, my lord: let her wear it out with good counsel.	**CLAUDIO** We must never tell him, my lord. Rather let her passion burn itself out
LEONATO Nay, that's impossible: she may wear her heart out first.	**LEONATO** No - that won't happen: she will burn her heart out first
DON PEDRO Well, we will hear further of it by your daughter: let it cool the while. I love Benedick well; and I could wish he would modestly examine himself, to see how much he is unworthy so good a lady.	**DON PEDRO** OK - so we'll put the plan on hold and wait for more information from Hero. I'm very fond of Benedick and I wish he would have a good, hard look at himself and see that he'd actually be very lucky to have such a good woman for a wife.
LEONATO My lord, will you walk? dinner is ready.	**LEONATO** Shall we go, my Lord? Dinner is ready.
CLAUDIO If he do not dote on her upon this, I will never trust my expectation.	**CLAUDIO** *(quietly, to DON PEDRO and LEONATO)* If this doesn't make him fall for her, I'll never trust my judgement again.
DON PEDRO Let there be the same net spread for her; and that must your daughter and her gentlewomen carry. The sport will be, when they hold one an opinion of another's dotage, and no such matter: that's the scene that I would see, which will be merely a dumb-show. Let us send her to call him in to dinner.	**DON PEDRO** *(quietly to LEONATO)* We'll cast the same net for Beatrice - your daughter and her companion must do it. The fun will really start when they both believe the other loves them, though of course that's not true. That's what I'm looking forward to seeing - and I mean *seeing*, as they'll both be struck dumb. Let's send Beatrice to call Benedick in to dinner.

Exeunt DON PEDRO, CLAUDIO, and LEONATO	*DON PEDRO, CLAUDIO, and LEONATO exit*
BENEDICK This can be no trick: the conference was sadly borne. They have the truth of this from Hero. They seem to pity the lady: it seems her affections have their full bent. Love me! why, it must be requited. I hear how I am censured: they say I will bear myself proudly, if I perceive the love come from her; they say too that she will rather die than give any sign of affection. I did never think to marry: I must not seem proud: happy are they that hear their detractions and can put them to mending. They say the lady is fair; 'tis a truth, I can bear them witness; and virtuous; 'tis so, I cannot reprove it; and wise, but for loving me; by my troth, it is no addition to her wit, nor no great argument of her folly, for I will be horribly in love with her. I may chance have some odd quirks and remnants of wit broken on me, because I have railed so long against marriage: but doth not the appetite alter? a man loves the meat in his youth that he cannot endure in his age. Shall quips and sentences and these paper bullets of the brain awe a man from the career of his humour? No, the world must be peopled. When I said I would die a bachelor, I did not think I should live till I were married. Here comes Beatrice. By this day! she's a fair lady: I do spy some marks of love in her.	**BENEDICK** *(Coming forward)* There's no way this is a trick: they weren't giggling at all, but quite serious. And they have Hero's testimony too. In fact they seemed to feel sorry for Beatrice: it seems she's totally infatuated. She loves me! Well, that love must be returned. I hear how they criticize me: they say I'll be really smug, if I think she loves me. They also said she'd rather die that show me any sign of affection. I never expected to get married: I mustn't blow my chance by seeming smug. It's a fortunate person who can take criticism and mend his ways as a result. They say she is beautiful: I can witness to that: and virtuous - that's true: I have no evidence to the contrary. And clever, except in loving me, which is no great advertisement for her cleverness, but it won't be proof of her foolishness, as I will be horribly in love with her. I might get a bit of flak here and there because I've been so anti-marriage so long, but can't tastes change? The meat a man loves in his youth he might detest in old age. Should wisecracks and old sayings and stinging words scare a man out of doing what he wants? No, the world needs to be populated. When I said I would die a bachelor I just meant that I didn't think I'd live to be married. Here comes Beatrice. She looks stunning! I think I see the signs of love in her.
Enter BEATRICE	*Enter BEATRICE*
BEATRICE Against my will I am sent to bid you come in to dinner.	**BEATRICE** Against my will, I have been sent to call you for dinner.
BENEDICK Fair Beatrice, I thank you for your pains.	**BENEDICK** My lovely Beatrice, I thank you for your pains.
BEATRICE I took no more pains for those thanks than you take pains to thank me: if it had been painful, I would not have come.	**BEATRICE** I took no more pains to get your thanks than you took pains to thank me. If it had been painful, I wouldn't have done it.
BENEDICK You take pleasure then in the message?	**BENEDICK** So you take pleasure in bringing me the message?
BEATRICE Yea, just so much as you may take upon a knife's point and choke a daw withal. You have no stomach, signior: fare you well.	**BEATRICE** Yes, about as much as you could fit on the point of a knife, and choke a foolish bird with. If you're not hungry, sir, I'll say goodbye.
Exit	*She exits*

BENEDICK Ha! 'Against my will I am sent to bid you come in to dinner;' there's a double meaning in that 'I took no more pains for those thanks than you took pains to thank me.' that's as much as to say, Any pains that I take for you is as easy as thanks. If I do not take pity of her, I am a villain; if I do not love her, I am a Jew. I will go get her picture. *Exit*	**BENEDICK** Ha! 'Against my will, I have been sent to call you for dinner' - there's a double meaning in that. 'I took no more pains to get your thanks than you took pains to thank me ' - what she's really saying is, 'Doing anything for you is as easy as saying thank-you'. I'd have to be a really odd person not to take pity on her; and have a heart of stone not to love her. I will go and get a miniature of her made as a sign of love. *He exits*

Analysis of Act 2 Scene 3

This is a 'split screen scene: the audience sees both Benedick and those he is eavesdropping on. They know what Benedick does not: that this is a set-up, aimed at getting him to believe Beatrice is in love with him so that he will reveal his love for Beatrice.

Summary:
Sitting alone in the orchard, Benedick ponders the sudden change in Claudio from soldier to lover. He hopes that he will keep managing to resist falling in love himself, because he thinks men in love are fools – they are like wobbly jelly or oysters. This gets him thinking about the kind of woman he might like to marry if one existed who had all the characteristics he demands.

While he's enjoying his thoughts – which he shares with the audience as a 'thinking aloud' **soliloquy** – Claudio, Don Pedro and Leonato enter, so Benedick decides to hide to overhear their conversation. However, the trio know where he is hiding and they intend fabricating [making up] a conversation purposely for him to hear.

To string things out, they've arranged for Balthasar to sing them a song about how men deceive women – Benedick is not impressed by the song. Hearing about 'the fraud of men' seems to spark conversation about a supposed previous conversation in which Leonato revealed that Beatrice was in love with Benedick.

Claudio reports back to the group about how Benedick is reacting using country metaphors to do with trapping birds and catching fish. Benedick believes the story Leonato tells of Hero's love because he feels sure Leonato is too old and serious to be involved in trickery.

In the overheard conversation, the strength and desperation of Beatrice's love for Benedick is contrasted with the horror she has of Benedick discovering it because he will mock her. Don Pedro says he wishes Beatrice were in love with him. Although they list Benedick's good points, Don Pedro manages to turn these into insults and on the strength of these characteristics the trio decide it would harm Beatrice to tell Benedick of her love – instead Hero should tell her to forget about him.

As they leave the orchard, Don Pedro says they should get Hero to play the same trick on Beatrice; meanwhile, they'll send Beatrice to call Benedick in for dinner.

Partly because he has heard that Hero told her father of it, Benedick believes that Beatrice must be in love with him, so decides to return her feelings. He changes his mind about marriage, saying 'the world must be peopled [populated]', despite knowing that he will be teased mercilessly.
When she comes to call Benedick in for dinner, Beatrice is abrupt and aggressive, yet Benedick is convinced she's definitely showing clear signs of love.

Genre:
Overheard conversation is a favourite device in Shakespeare's plays, particularly in his comedies. [It is still a stock trick in modern comedies]The stage on which the plays were performed had two handy pillars with were ideal for hiding behind in such a way that the audience could see the actor, who ducked away again at key moments. Productions have lots of fun inventing places for Benedick to hide while listening to the conversation and, of course, responding to the news of Beatrice's supposed love.

Structure:
This scene begins with Benedick justifying his decision to remain a bachelor and ends with him justifying his decision to return Beatrice's love.

Throughout the scene he has been speaking in prose, but the two lines Benedick addresses to Beatrice are almost in **blank verse** [unrhymed lines of ten syllables, with a repeated pattern of unstressed and stressed, also known as **iambic pentameter**], as if he is trying to use elevated [higher/posher] 'love' language to her.

Themes:

- Appearance vs. reality

Benedick is convinced he has overheard something that was meant to be kept secret from him, while the audience knows that he is falling into a trap and is meant to overhear the conversation. When the audience knows something a character does not, it is called **dramatic irony**. Another example of dramatic irony occurs when Beatrice comes to call Benedick. The audience knows why Benedick is behaving strangely, but she does not; the audience also knows that she has not been dying of love for Benedick, so that there are no 'marks of love' for Benedick to spy in her, even though he is convinced he does.

Language:
When Claudio says, '...stalk on, stalk on the fowl sits' he is using the image of a hunter stalking a game bird; Benedick is a 'sitting duck' unable to escape, so definitely hearing what they say. Giving the next update, Claudio says, 'Bait the hook well, this fish will bite', suggesting he'll fall for the trick 'hook, line and sinker'. As they leave, Don Pedro uses another image related to 'catching' when he says 'let there be the same net spread for her' – watch for similarly thematic imagery.

Act 3 Scene 1

ORIGINAL TEXT	MODERN TRANSLATION
LEONATO'S garden.	**LEONATO'S garden.**
Enter HERO, MARGARET, and URSULA	*HERO, MARGARET, and URSULA enter*
HERO Good Margaret, run thee to the parlor; There shalt thou find my cousin Beatrice Proposing with the prince and Claudio: Whisper her ear and tell her, I and Ursula Walk in the orchard and our whole discourse Is all of her; say that thou overheard'st us; And bid her steal into the pleached bower, Where honeysuckles, ripen'd by the sun, Forbid the sun to enter, like favourites, Made proud by princes, that advance their pride Against that power that bred it: there will she hide her, To listen our purpose. This is thy office; Bear thee well in it and leave us alone.	**HERO** Margaret, run to the sitting-room: you'll find my cousin Beatrice there, talking to Claudio and the Prince. Whisper to her that Ursula and I are walking in the orchard and our whole conversation is about her - say that you overheard us - and tell her she should sneak into the avenue where the intertwined branches of honeysuckle have grown so thick that they block out the sunlight - like courtiers who have grown powerful in the favour of a prince and then plotted against him - and hide there to listen to our conversation. That's your job - do it well, and then leave us alone.
MARGARET I'll make her come, I warrant you, presently.	**MARGARET** I'll make her come right away I promise.
Exit	*She exits*
HERO Now, Ursula, when Beatrice doth come, As we do trace this alley up and down, Our talk must only be of Benedick. When I do name him, let it be thy part To praise him more than ever man did merit: My talk to thee must be how Benedick Is sick in love with Beatrice. Of this matter Is little Cupid's crafty arrow made, That only wounds by hearsay.	**HERO** Now, Ursula, when Beatrice comes, and we're walking up and down the avenue, we must be talking only about Benedick. When I mention his name, you must praise him more highly than any man deserves: My talk to you will be all about how love-sick Benedick is for Beatrice. Overheard gossip is the stuff Cupid's clever little arrows are made of.
Enter BEATRICE, behind	*BEATRICE enters, behind them*
Now begin; For look where Beatrice, like a lapwing, runs Close by the ground, to hear our conference.	Let's start - Beatrice is just running over, keeping low like a bird pretending to be injured, to listen in on our conversation.
URSULA The pleasant'st angling is to see the fish Cut with her golden oars the silver stream, And greedily devour the treacherous bait: So angle we for Beatrice; who even now Is couched in the woodbine coverture. Fear you not my part of the dialogue.	**URSULA** The best angling is when you actually see the fish cut through the silver water with its golden fins And greedily take the bait. That's how it will be with Beatrice, who's already crouching in the shade of the honeysuckle. Don't worry - I'll play my part well.

HERO Then go we near her, that her ear lose nothing Of the false sweet bait that we lay for it. *Approaching the bower* No, truly, Ursula, she is too disdainful; I know her spirits are as coy and wild As haggerds of the rock.	**HERO** Then let's move closer so she doesn't miss a word of the sweet bait we're setting for her ... *(Approaching the bower, speaking more loudly)* No, really, Ursula, she's too scornful - she's as skittish and fierce as the wild hawks of the rocks
URSULA But are you sure That Benedick loves Beatrice so entirely?	**URSULA** But are you sure that Benedick is utterly in love with Beatrice?
HERO So says the prince and my new-trothed lord.	**HERO** That's what the prince and my new fiancé say.
URSULA And did they bid you tell her of it, madam?	**URSULA** And did they ask you to tell Beatrice about it, madam?
HERO They did entreat me to acquaint her of it; But I persuaded them, if they loved Benedick, To wish him wrestle with affection, And never to let Beatrice know of it.	**HERO** They begged me to tell her, but I persuaded them that if they really loved Benedick then they should tell him to get a grip on himself and never breathe a word of it to Beatrice.
URSULA Why did you so? Doth not the gentleman Deserve as full as fortunate a bed As ever Beatrice shall couch upon?	**URSULA** Why did you do that? Doesn't Benedick deserve some marital bliss?
HERO O god of love! I know he doth deserve As much as may be yielded to a man: But Nature never framed a woman's heart Of prouder stuff than that of Beatrice; Disdain and scorn ride sparkling in her eyes, Misprising what they look on, and her wit Values itself so highly that to her All matter else seems weak: she cannot love, Nor take no shape nor project of affection, She is so self-endeared.	**HERO** By the god of love, he deserves as much as any man is allowed! But Nature never made any woman's heart out of prouder material than it did Beatrice's. You can see her eyes sparkle with pleasure as they scorn and despise everything they look at. And she's so full of her own cleverness that she's not interested in anything else - and she's so in love with herself that she's not interested in anybody else!
URSULA Sure, I think so; And therefore certainly it were not good She knew his love, lest she make sport at it.	**URSULA** Maybe you're right - it wouldn't be good if she knew that Benedick loves her - she'd just make fun of him.
HERO Why, you speak truth. I never yet saw man, How wise, how noble, young, how rarely featured, But she would spell him backward: if fair-faced, She would swear the gentleman should be her sister; If black, why, Nature, drawing of an antique, Made a foul blot; if tall, a lance ill-headed;	**HERO** It's true. I've yet to see a man so clever, so noble, so youthful, so handsome that she wouldn't turn it all back to front and make him look bad. If his skin is fair, she'd say he looked like a girl, if swarthy, then Nature must have made an ink-blot while drawing a buffoon. If tall, then he's a wonky-headed lance, if short a

If low, an agate very vilely cut; If speaking, why, a vane blown with all winds; If silent, why, a block moved with none. So turns she every man the wrong side out And never gives to truth and virtue that Which simpleness and merit purchaseth.	badly carved miniature; if talkative he's a weathervane, turning to face whatever wind blows, if he doesn't talk, then he's a solid block, not moved by the wind at all. So she turns everybody's character on its head and never acknowledges integrity or merit in a man.
URSULA Sure, sure, such carping is not commendable.	**URSULA** It's true - that constant nitpicking is not something to admire.
HERO No, not to be so odd and from all fashions As Beatrice is, cannot be commendable: But who dare tell her so? If I should speak, She would mock me into air; O, she would laugh me Out of myself, press me to death with wit. Therefore let Benedick, like cover'd fire, Consume away in sighs, waste inwardly: It were a better death than die with mocks, Which is as bad as die with tickling.	**HERO** It's certainly not admirable to be such a perverse oddball as Beatrice is. But who's got the courage to tell her? If I said anything she'd laugh me out of court she would mock me till I disappeared into thin air - she'd laugh me right out of my body, then crush me with her wit. Rather let Benedick be like a covered fire that smoulders away unseen until it uses up all the air and die than die of mockery, which is a bad as being tickled to death.
URSULA Yet tell her of it: hear what she will say.	**URSULA** I still wonder if you shouldn't tell her and hear what she has to say.
HERO No; rather I will go to Benedick And counsel him to fight against his passion. And, truly, I'll devise some honest slanders To stain my cousin with: one doth not know How much an ill word may empoison liking.	**HERO** No. I'll rather go to Benedick and advise him to fight his feelings. I'll also make up a few horrible things about Beatrice. A relationship can be poisoned more easily than you think by a single nasty word.
URSULA O, do not do your cousin such a wrong. She cannot be so much without true judgment-- Having so swift and excellent a wit As she is prized to have--as to refuse So rare a gentleman as Signior Benedick.	**URSULA** Oh - don't do such an awful thing to your cousin! She can't be so stupid - having the a quick and clever mind that everybody says she does- that she'd refuse such a special gentleman as Sir Benedick.
HERO He is the only man of Italy. Always excepted my dear Claudio.	**HERO** He's the only worthy man in the whole of Italy - with the exception of my dear Claudio, of course.
URSULA I pray you, be not angry with me, madam, Speaking my fancy: Signior Benedick, For shape, for bearing, argument and valour, Goes foremost in report through Italy.	**URSULA** Please don't be angry with me for speaking my mind, madam, but Sir Benedick is considered the best man in Italy for looks, bearing, reasoning and bravery.
HERO Indeed, he hath an excellent good name.	**HERO** He does indeed have a very good reputation.
URSULA His excellence did earn it, ere he had it. When are you married, madam?	**URSULA** And he has earned it, right from the start. When are you going to be married, madam?

HERO Why, every day, to-morrow. Come, go in: I'll show thee some attires, and have thy counsel Which is the best to furnish me to-morrow.	**HERO** Every single day - starting tomorrow. Come, let's go in and I'll show some dresses: you can advise me on which is the best one to wear tomorrow.
URSULA She's limed, I warrant you: we have caught her, madam.	**URSULA** *(quietly to Hero)* She's in the trap, madam. I'm sure we've caught her.
HERO If it proves so, then loving goes by haps: Some Cupid kills with arrows, some with traps.	**HERO** If so, then love is a game of chance. Cupid gets some with his arrows, but others he catches in traps.
Exeunt HERO and URSULA	*HERO and URSULA both exit*
BEATRICE [Coming forward] What fire is in mine ears? Can this be true? Stand I condemn'd for pride and scorn so much? Contempt, farewell! and maiden pride, adieu! No glory lives behind the back of such. And, Benedick, love on; I will requite thee, Taming my wild heart to thy loving hand: If thou dost love, my kindness shall incite thee To bind our loves up in a holy band; For others say thou dost deserve, and I Believe it better than reportingly.	**BEATRICE** *(Coming forward)* These words burn me like fire! Can this be true? Can I be so condemned for my pride and scornfulness? Then I'll say goodbye to contemptuousness, and to my pride in being unmarried! I'm not well spoken of behind my back for being like that. And, Benedick, keep on loving me - I will return your love: I'll no longer be a wild hawk but a tame one, coming to your loving hand. I'll be so kind towards you that If you really do love me, then you will be encouraged to tie the knot. Others say that you deserve my love, and I believe it's true - even more so than what they say.
Exit	She exits

Analysis of Act 3 Scene 1

This is the companion scene to the previous one; here Beatrice is led to believe she's overhearing a private conversation: the hot gossip that Benedick loves Beatrice, but dare not tell her for fear of being mocked.

Summary:
The scene opens with Hero sending Margaret to tell Beatrice she's being gossiped about by Hero and Ursula in the arbour – a sheltered area in the garden covered with climbing plants and shrubs, where Beatrice can easily 'hide'. Hero makes sure she will overhear the conversation and tells Ursula what to say.
Their story is that Don Pedro and Claudio are convinced that Benedick loves Beatrice and want to tell her, but Hero has advised her not to because Beatrice will break any man down by mocking him. They praise Benedick and imagine how cruel Beatrice would be to him if she knew of his love: it would be better, they decide, if Benedick were told to forget Beatrice. They end off by saying how highly thought of Benedick is in Italy to emphasise what a catch he would be, then change the subject to Hero's wedding plans as they walk off to choose her dress.

Left alone, the stunned Beatrice thinks about the bad reputation her 'wit' has earned her. She reconsiders her attitude and decides to change her mind about Benedick and marriage. 'I will requite thee' she says to the imagined Benedick.

Genre:
A common thread in Shakespeare's comedies is that the lovers reach an awareness of themselves and the person they love, and changing as the situation demands. As Benedick has done in the previous scene, Beatrice hears her friends list her faults and admits they are speaking the truth. She hears them praise Benedick's virtues and claim that he has a good reputation and admits what they say is true and so decides to change, to tame her 'wild heart'.

Form:
While the men spoke in prose [i.e. sentences, 'normal'] when tricking Benedick, the women speak in blank verse, indicating a more elevated form of speaking. Only about 28% of the play is written in verse, so it is worth noticing when characters use it. We don't know why Shakespeare used verse here, but it may indicate [show/ suggest] that the men are just having a bit of fun, trying to get Benedick to eat his words and get married after all. Whereas for the women, marriage is a serious things and they really do want to help Beatrice overcome her resistance to it.
Similarly, Benedick speaks in prose when reviewing the revelation in his soliloquy and Beatrice moves up to verse after overhearing that Benedick loves her. In fact, though only 10 lines, Beatrice's speech is very like a sonnet in rhyme scheme, suggesting she is very much in love.

Structure:
The whole play features pairs, opposites, balances: two pairs of lovers, opposite in disposition and expectation; two brothers, one caring and forgiving, one a villain; two weddings and two sets of deception. This scene is one of a pair, the counterpart to Benedick's being tricked into realising his love for Beatrice, where Beatrice, overhearing that Benedick loves her, decided to return his love. We could call this a positive deception, as the point of it is to bring about a reconciliation between the two sparring partners.

Language:
As with Benedick's deception, countryside imagery is used in this scene to comment on Beatrice's gullibility in believing the ruse. She is described as a 'lapwing' a bird that darts along in short runs,

then seems to freeze before running on again. Similarly, after the bird imagery comes the fishing metaphor: 'The pleasantest angling is to see the fish/ Cut with her golden oars the silver stream,/ And greedily devour the treacherous bait.' When Ursula later reports: 'She's limed I warrant you, we have caught her, madam' she is saying they've trapped Beatrice. Using birdlime – a white calcium powder - was a way of ensnaring or trapping birds. Compare this to Act 2 scene3; again Shakespeare uses a bird, a hooked fish and a trap to describe the eavesdropper being lured to listen to the conversation set up to trick them into recognising their feelings for what they are.

Themes:

- Love

The play explores two types of love: admiration or infatuation as represented by Hero and Claudio who hardly speak to one another, and the 'tried and tested, relationship based on a 'warts and all' knowledge such as Beatrice and Benedick have of one another. Claudio and Hero follow the conventional procedures of aristocratic [noble /upper class] Elizabethan courtship: wooing by a representative of the groom, negotiation and settlement of the dowry, a formal betrothal and finally a wedding ceremony. As individuals these characters also represent the Elizabethan ideal of an honourable, noble soldier and a beautiful, 'modest' heiress. On the other hand, Beatrice and Benedick are far from the ideal – they're both individuals, too opinionated and outspoken, with no tolerance for hypocrisy. It has been said that their relationship embodies what Shakespeare – in one of his sonnets – calls 'a marriage of true minds'.

Context:

Shakespeare often used well known stories as the basis for his plays. The tale of a man thinking his betrothed is unfaithful because a man is seen at her window was centuries old in Elizabethan times and many versions of it already existed – a bit like fairy tales today. So Claudio and Hero's story is an old one, but Beatrice and Benedick seem to be Shakespeare's own creation. Perhaps this is why Claudio and Hero have a 'traditional' relationship, whereas Beatrice and Benedick have – particularly to an Elizabethan audience – a 'modern' love story.

Act 3 Scene 2

ORIGINAL TEXT	MODERN TRANSLATION
A room in LEONATO'S house	**A room in LEONATO'S house**
Enter DON PEDRO, CLAUDIO, BENEDICK, and LEONATO	*DON PEDRO, CLAUDIO, BENEDICK, and LEONATO enter*
DON PEDRO I do but stay till your marriage be consummate, and then go I toward Arragon.	**DON PEDRO** I'll stay until your marriage is legally complete, then make for Arragon.
CLAUDIO I'll bring you thither, my lord, if you'll vouchsafe me.	**CLAUDIO** I'll accompany you, my lord, if you'll allow me.
DON PEDRO Nay, that would be as great a soil in the new gloss of your marriage as to show a child his new coat and forbid him to wear it. I will only be bold with Benedick for his company; for, from the crown of his head to the sole of his foot, he is all mirth: he hath twice or thrice cut Cupid's bow-string and the little hangman dare not shoot at him; he hath a heart as sound as a bell and his tongue is the clapper, for what his heart thinks his tongue speaks.	**DON PEDRO** No - that would spoil the shine of your new marriage - it would be like showing a child a new coat then saying he mustn't wear it! I'll ask only Benedick to come with me - he's a bundle of fun from head to toe, and he's already cut Cupid's bow string two or three times, so that there's no danger that the little rascal will try to make him fall in love with somebody - and his heart is like a bell, with his tongue like the clapper, so he speaks whatever is in his heart.
BENEDICK Gallants, I am not as I have been.	**BENEDICK** Gentlemen, I am not the person I used to be.
LEONATO So say I, methinks you are sadder.	**LEONATO** I agree: I think you are more serious
CLAUDIO I hope he be in love.	**CLAUDIO** I hope he's in love.
DON PEDRO Hang him, truant! there's no true drop of blood in him, to be truly touched with love: if he be sad, he wants money.	**DON PEDRO** Come off it! There's no sincere blood in him that could be sincerely affected by love: if he looks serious, it's because he's short of money.
BENEDICK I have the toothache.	**BENEDICK** I have a toothache.
DON PEDRO Draw it.	**DON PEDRO** Draw it.
BENEDICK Hang it!	**BENEDICK** Hang it!
CLAUDIO You must hang it first, and draw it afterwards.	**CLAUDIO** You must hang it first, and then draw it.
DON PEDRO What! sigh for the toothache?	**DON PEDRO** What? Is all this moaning because of a toothache?

LEONATO Where is but a humour or a worm.	**LEONATO** That must be caused either by an imbalance in the body's humours, or by an infection.
BENEDICK Well, everyone can master a grief but he that has it.	**BENEDICK** Well, everyone can deal with pain except the person who's actually experiencing it.
CLAUDIO Yet say I, he is in love.	**CLAUDIO** I tell you, he's in love.
DON PEDRO There is no appearance of fancy in him, unless it be a fancy that he hath to strange disguises; as, to be a Dutchman today, a Frenchman to-morrow, or in the shape of two countries at once, as, a German from the waist downward, all slops, and a Spaniard from the hip upward, no doublet. Unless he have a fancy to this foolery, as it appears he hath, he is no fool for fancy, as you would have it appear he is.	**DON PEDRO** There's no obvious signs of love in him - unless you count the love he has for dressing in strange costumes - so as to look like a Dutchman today, a Frenchman tomorrow - or even two countries at once: like a German from the waist down, with his baggy trousers and a Spaniard from hips up, with no jacket. Unless he you mean he has a love for this kind of foolishness, which his appearance indeed suggests he has, then he is not a fool for love as you claim he is.
CLAUDIO If he be not in love with some woman, there is no believing old signs: a' brushes his hat o' mornings; what should that bode?	**CLAUDIO** If he's not in love with a woman then you can't trust the usual symptoms: he brushes his hat in the mornings - what do you suppose that means?
DON PEDRO Hath any man seen him at the barber's?	**DON PEDRO** Has anyone seen him at the barber's?
CLAUDIO No, but the barber's man hath been seen with him, and the old ornament of his cheek hath already stuffed tennis-balls.	**CLAUDIO** No, but the barber's assistant has been seen with him - and the beard-hair that used to decorate his cheeks has already been used to stuff tennis balls.
LEONATO Indeed, he looks younger than he did, by the loss of a beard.	**LEONATO** He looks younger without a beard.
DON PEDRO Nay, a' rubs himself with civet: can you smell him out by that?	**DON PEDRO** Not just that - he rubs perfume on himself - can you smell out his secret now?
CLAUDIO That's as much as to say, the sweet youth's in love.	**CLAUDIO** That as good as confirms the dear boy is in love.
DON PEDRO The greatest note of it is his melancholy.	**DON PEDRO** The biggest clue is his seriousness.
CLAUDIO And when was he wont to wash his face?	**CLAUDIO** And when was he known to wash his face?
DON PEDRO Yea, or to paint himself? for the which, I hear what they say of him.	**DON PEDRO** Yes, or to wear make-up? I hear what people are saying about him for doing that.

CLAUDIO Nay, but his jesting spirit; which is now crept into a lute-string and now governed by stops.	**CLAUDIO** And what about his free and mocking spirit? It now seems he can be played like a lute.
DON PEDRO Indeed, that tells a heavy tale for him: conclude, conclude he is in love.	**DON PEDRO** Indeed, this is a great weight of evidence. The conclusion must be that he is in love.
CLAUDIO Nay, but I know who loves him.	**CLAUDIO** And I know who loves him.
DON PEDRO That would I know too: I warrant, one that knows him not.	**DON PEDRO** I'd like to know that too. It must be somebody who doesn't know him.
CLAUDIO Yes, and his ill conditions; and, in despite of all, dies for him.	**CLAUDIO** Yes, she knows him, and knows all his bad qualities, and despite all that she's still dying to be with him.
DON PEDRO She shall be buried with her face upwards.	**DON PEDRO** She'll be buried with her face upwards then.
BENEDICK Yet is this no charm for the toothache. Old signior, walk aside with me: I have studied eight or nine wise words to speak to you, which these hobby-horses must not hear.	**BENEDICK** But none of this banter cures my toothache. *(To Leonato)* Old sir, come walk with me: I have a few carefully considered words to speak to you, which I don't want to say in front of these clowns.
Exeunt BENEDICK and LEONATO	*BENEDICK and LEONATO both exit*
DON PEDRO For my life, to break with him about Beatrice.	**DON PEDRO** I'd bet my life on it that he's gone to speak to him about Beatrice.
CLAUDIO 'Tis even so. Hero and Margaret have by this played their parts with Beatrice; and then the two bears will not bite one another when they meet.	**CLAUDIO** I'm sure that's right. Hero and Margaret have done their bit with Beatrice by now, so the two bears won't bite each another when they meet.
Enter DON JOHN	*DON JOHN enters*
DON JOHN My lord and brother, God save you!	**DON JOHN** My lord and brother, God save you!
DON PEDRO Good e'en, brother.	**DON PEDRO** Good evening, brother.
DON JOHN If your leisure served, I would speak with you.	**DON JOHN** I would like to talk to you if you're not busy.
DON PEDRO In private?	**DON PEDRO** In private?
DON JOHN If it please you: yet Count Claudio may hear; for what I would speak of concerns him.	**DON JOHN** If you wouldn't mind - although Count Claudio can hear, because what I have to say concerns him.

DON PEDRO What's the matter?	**DON PEDRO** What's do you want to talk to us about?
DON JOHN [To CLAUDIO] Means your lordship to be married to-morrow?	**DON JOHN** (To CLAUDIO) Are you intending to get married tomorrow?
DON PEDRO You know he does.	**DON PEDRO** You know he is.
DON JOHN I know not that, when he knows what I know.	**DON JOHN** I do not know he is, not when he knows what I know.
CLAUDIO If there be any impediment, I pray you discover it.	**CLAUDIO** If there be any reason I should not marry her, please tell me.
DON JOHN You may think I love you not: let that appear hereafter, and aim better at me by that I now will manifest. For my brother, I think he holds you well, and in dearness of heart hath holp to effect your ensuing marriage;--surely suit ill spent and labour ill bestowed.	**DON JOHN** You may think I don't like you: I hope you will think better of me because of what I am about to tell you. For my brother's part, I believe he has a high opinion of you, and because of his affection for you, he has helped to bring about your forthcoming marriage -- surely a misguided effort.
DON PEDRO Why, what's the matter?	**DON PEDRO** Why, what's wrong?
DON JOHN I came hither to tell you; and, circumstances shortened, for she has been too long a talking of- the lady is disloyal.	**DON JOHN** I came here to tell you. To cut a long story short, as she has already been spoken of too long: the lady is unfaithful.
CLAUDIO Who, Hero?	**CLAUDIO** Who, Hero?
DON PEDRO Even she; Leonato's Hero, your Hero, every man's Hero.	**DON PEDRO** Yes, Hero: Leonato's Hero, your Hero, every man's Hero.
CLAUDIO Disloyal?	**CLAUDIO** Unfaithful?
DON JOHN The word is too good to paint out her wickedness; I could say she were worse: think you of a worse title, and I will fit her to it. Wonder not till further warrant: go but with me to-night, you shall see her chamber-window entered, even the night before her wedding-day: if you love her then, to-morrow wed her; but it would better fit your honour to change your mind.	**DON JOHN** The word hardly covers the extent of her wickedness. She is worse than unfaithful. Think of something worse to call her and I'll show it fits her. But don't try to work out what I mean, wait for the evidence: come with me tonight and you'll see somebody enter through her bedroom window - the very night before her wedding! If you still love her after that, go ahead and marry her - but honour would be better served if you changed your mind.

CLAUDIO May this be so?	**CLAUDIO** Is this possible?
DON PEDRO I will not think it.	**DON PEDRO** I refuse to believe it.
DON JOHN If you dare not trust that you see, confess not that you know: if you will follow me, I will show you enough; and when you have seen more and heard more, proceed accordingly.	**DON JOHN** If you don't dare to risk seeing what she gets up to, then don't claim to know her. If you follow me, I'll give you all the proof you need. Once you've got that, then you can decide what to do.
CLAUDIO If I see anything to-night why I should not marry her to-morrow in the congregation, where I should wed, there will I shame her.	**CLAUDIO** If I see anything tonight that convinces me I shouldn't marry her tomorrow I will shame her in front of the very congregation who came to see us married.
DON PEDRO And, as I wooed for thee to obtain her, I will join with thee to disgrace her.	**DON PEDRO** And, just as I helped you court her, I will help you disgrace her.
DON JOHN I will disparage her no farther till you are my witnesses: bear it coldly but till midnight, and let the issue show itself.	**DON JOHN** I won't say any more bad things about her until you can see for yourselves. Keep your cool until midnight, then events can speak for themselves.
DON PEDRO O day untowardly turned!	**DON PEDRO** Today has turned into a disaster!
CLAUDIO O mischief strangely thwarting!	**CLAUDIO** This unexpected evil deed has ruined our plans!
DON JOHN O plague right well prevented! so will you say when you have seen the sequel.	**DON JOHN** It's a disaster you were lucky to avoid! That's what you'll tell yourselves when you've seen what follows.
Exeunt	*They all leave*

Analysis of Act 3 Scene 2

This scene begins with happy banter as his friends tease Benedick about being in love, but ends gloomily as Don John puts his plan to discredit Hero into action.

Summary:
With a lot of teasing and joking, Claudio and Don Pedro – with the occasional comment from Leonato- are trying to get Benedick to admit that he is in love, hinting that they know who he is in love with too. He seems about to tell them: 'Gallants, I am not as I have been', but changes his mind and instead claims to have toothache.*

Despite his friends making jokes at his expense, Benedick asks to speak to Leonato in private: to an Elizabethan audience it would be obvious that the 'wise words' his friends, the 'hobby-horses' couldn't hear, are him asking for Beatrice's hand in marriage. Just in case they didn't pick up the clue, Don Pedro spells it out: to 'break with him' means to 'broker' or negotiate the terms of the marriage.

This rowdy mood changes instantly when Don John comes in. His seemingly silly questions create tension, because both Claudio and Don Pedro sense something is not being said, which makes them apprehensive [uneasy]. When Don John claims he has proof of Hero's unfaithfulness, even inviting them to witness her disloyal behaviour, Claudio promises to shame her in front of the congregation at the wedding the next day and Don Pedro promises to help him.

From laughing at how Benedick has fallen into their 'trap', Claudio and Don Pedro end the scene in Don John's trap.

Genre:
Wordplay, puns, allusions [references] and insinuations are all elements of comedy and in their exuberance [excitement/ high spirits/ exhilaration] the friends use all these to tease Benedick – *see* ***Language.*** When Don John sets his trap, the insinuations are not comic, they suggest without spelling out the lie he wants Claudio to believe. Don Pedro and Claudio care more about their honour than Hero's and so to vindicate themselves want to humiliate her in front of the congregation.

In Shakespeare's comedies, a harsh 'law' or set of social rules is often undermined by the younger generation and here it seems to be the concept of marriage as merely an alliance: if Claudio had known Hero as well as Benedick knows Beatrice, he would have had it out with her first and learned the truth before the wedding.

Context:
Elizabethan society was **patriarchal**, meaning men [especially fathers] dominated society. Women had to submit to their husbands as legally they were their property. In a way, they were pawns in a male game. Despite the fact that Queen Elizabeth I was on the throne at the time and showed herself as capable, educated and politically astute [shrewd/ smart/ perceptive] as any man, Elizabethan men used several stereotypes of women to justify their control over them.

We've previously mentioned the high value set on a virgin bride to ensure at least the heir truly belongs to the father. If an heiress like Hero was proved unchaste [impure/ immoral/sinful] she would lose her inheritance – so Don John's accusation is much more powerful than it would be to modern audiences.

A woman had to be a 'goddess', perfect in every way; courtly love demanded that she was placed on a metaphorical pedestal [stand/ plinth] and worshipped – perhaps that is why Queen Elizabeth herself covered her face in lead powder to make herself look white as marble: like a statue. So far, Hero has fitted this stereotype, admired from afar by Claudio.

The stereotype Beatrice has fitted is woman as a shrew who needs taming, the fate of any woman who might try to speak for herself. Maybe this is why Don Pedro feels she needs a husband.

If a woman didn't belong to a man, the assumption was that she must be a prostitute, available to be bought. People knew that all women were bought and sold, but society pretended the dowry arrangements were different, that marriage was sacred.

Language:
The exploits of **Cupid** have been an ongoing – **sustained/ extended- metaphor** for love throughout the play. You could say Cupid – as god of desire/ erotic love – is **symbolic** of falling in love, or a **personification** of love. You could also describe it as a **metonymy**, where a thing or concept – sexual desire or erotic love - is called not by its own name but rather by the name of something – Cupid- associated in meaning with it.

Benedick is undergoing the same change from soldier to lover that he teased Claudio for, so, as he knew they would, his friends are teasing him now. At first, Don Pedro claims that Cupid would never 'dare' shoot at Benedick because he has had his 'bow-string' cut twice – in other words Benedick has resisted falling in love several times and is now immune. Though Claudio insists he's in love, Don Pedro suggests he wants to borrow money, which is why he looks so serious; Benedick claims he has toothache. There are four references to toothache in this play, three of them in this scene. In Elizabethan times 'toothache could be a **euphemism** [neutral term] used by lovers to explain their moodiness. What follows is a joke on the term 'hanged, drawn (and quartered)', the regular punishment for traitors: Benedick is a 'traitor' to the cause of being a bachelor at sixty or till he dies.

Characters:

- Hero

As the conventional heroine, Hero is everything the Elizabethan audience wanted in a woman – wealthy, beautiful, modest and submissive, with the ideal lover waiting to wed her. She submits to what is expected of her, whereas Beatrice resists. First she is led to believe that Don Pedro woos her for himself – she will be a princess, that's what both her father and uncle have told her. Then it turns out she's being wooed for Claudio and she seems happy with that. Notice how she keeps submitting, despite what happens to her next.

Ironically, it is Hero who says she'll 'devise some honest slanders' – counter-balancing Don John's dishonest slanders about her – because 'an ill word may empoison liking', which is exactly the effect Don John's 'ill word' or slander is having on Claudio's 'liking' of her: poisoning it.

Think about Hero's character when the men aren't about: she shows herself as intelligent, lively and perceptive: Shakespeare shows that she is kept subservient by her social need to be submissive.

ORIGINAL TEXT	MODERN TRANSLATION
A street.	**A street.**
Enter DOGBERRY and VERGES with the Watch	*DOGBERRY and VERGES with recruits for the Prince's Night Watch*
DOGBERRY Are you good men and true?	**DOGBERRY** Are you all good and honest men?
VERGES Yea, or else it were pity but they should suffer salvation, body and soul.	**VERGES** They better be or, it's a pity, but they will suffer salvation, body and soul.
DOGBERRY Nay, that were a punishment too good for them, if they should have any allegiance in them, being chosen for the prince's watch.	**DOGBERRY** Nah, if they showed themselves to be loyal when chosen for the Prince's watch that would be a punishment too good for them.
VERGES Well, give them their charge, neighbour Dogberry.	**VERGES** Well, give them their commission, comrade Dogberry.
DOGBERRY First, who think you the most desertless man to be constable?	**DOGBERRY** First, do you think is the most ineligible man to be leader of the watch?
First Watchman Hugh Oatcake, sir, or George Seacole; for they can write and read.	**First Watchman** Hugh Oatcake, sir, or George Seacole: both of them can write and read.
DOGBERRY Come hither, neighbour Seacole. God hath blessed you with a good name: to be a well-favoured man is the gift of fortune; but to write and read comes by nature.	**DOGBERRY** Step forward, comrade Seacole. God has blessed you with a good name! To be a good-looking man is a matter of luck; but to write and read is a matter of nature.
Second Watchman Both which, master constable,-	**Second Watchman** Both of which, master constable,-
DOGBERRY You have: I knew it would be your answer. Well, for your favour, sir, why, give God thanks, and make no boast of it; and for your writing and reading, let that appear when there is no need of such vanity. You are thought here to be the most senseless and fit man for the constable of the watch; therefore bear you the lantern. This is your charge: you shall comprehend all vagrom men; you are to bid any man stand, in the prince's name.	**DOGBERRY** You have: I knew that would be your answer. Well, for your good looks, sir, give thanks to God, and don't take the credit for it. As for your reading and writing, use them when your looks aren't enough. You are considered the most senseless here, so you should be constable and carry the lantern. Your job is to comprehend any vagrants. You are to order these men to stop, in the Prince's name.
Second Watchman How if a' will not stand?	**Second Watchman** What if he doesn't stop?

DOGBERRY Why, then, take no note of him, but let him go; and presently call the rest of the watch together and thank God you are rid of a knave.	**DOGBERRY** Then you look the other way and let him escape - after which you can call the rest of the watch together and thank God you are rid of the scoundrel!
VERGES If he will not stand when he is bidden, he is none of the prince's subjects.	**VERGES** If he won't stop when he's told, you see, he obviously can't be one of the Prince's subjects.
DOGBERRY True, and they are to meddle with none but the prince's subjects. You shall also make no noise in the streets; for, for the watch to babble and to talk is most tolerable and not to be endured.	**DOGBERRY** That is true, and you must concern yourself only with the Prince's subjects. You must also not make a noise in the streets. For the members of the Watch to babble away is most tolerable and will not be permitted.
Watchman We will rather sleep than talk: we know what belongs to a watch.	**Watchman** We'll rather sleep than talk - we know what's appropriate to the Watch.
DOGBERRY Why, you speak like an ancient and most quiet watchman; for I cannot see how sleeping should offend: only, have a care that your bills be not stolen. Well, you are to call at all the ale-houses, and bid those that are drunk get them to bed.	**DOGBERRY** Why, you speak like a most experienced and quiet watchman. I see no harm in sleeping, but make sure your weapons don't get stolen. You are also to call at all the pubs, and instruct anybody who is drunk to go home to bed.
Watchman How if they will not?	**Watchman** What if they won't go?
DOGBERRY Why, then, let them alone till they are sober: if they make you not then the better answer, you may say they are not the men you took them for.	**DOGBERRY** Then you leave them until they have sobered up. If they still don't respond to your satisfaction, you tell them you must have the wrong man.
Watchman Well, sir.	**Watchman** Very well, sir.
DOGBERRY If you meet a thief, you may suspect him, by virtue of your office, to be no true man; and, for such kind of men, the less you meddle or make with them, why the more is for your honesty.	**DOGBERRY** If you meet a thief, you can't expect him to tell the truth to a member of the Watch. The less you have to do with such people, the better it is for your honesty.
Watchman If we know him to be a thief, shall we not lay hands on him?	**Watchman** If we know he's a thief, shouldn't we arrest him?
DOGBERRY Truly, by your office, you may; but I think they that touch pitch will be defiled: the most peaceable way for you, if you do take a thief, is to let him show himself what he is and steal out of your company.	**DOGBERRY** Certainly, as a member of the Watch, you may arrest him - but as I see it, if you put your hands in tar they will be contaminated by it. The most peaceable way to deal with a thief is to let him prove himself a thief by stealing away.

VERGES You have been always called a merciful man, partner.	**VERGES** You have always been known as a merciful man, partner.
DOGBERRY Truly, I would not hang a dog by my will, much more a man who hath any honesty in him.	**DOGBERRY** Truly, I would not willingly hang a dog, much more a man who has any honesty at all in him.
VERGES If you hear a child cry in the night, you must call to the nurse and bid her still it.	**VERGES** Next - If you hear a child crying in the night, you must call to its nurse and ask her to quieten it.
Watchman How if the nurse be asleep and will not hear us?	**Watchman** What if the nurse is asleep, and doesn't hear us?
DOGBERRY Why, then, depart in peace, and let the child wake her with crying; for the ewe that will not hear her lamb when it baes will never answer a calf when he bleats.	**DOGBERRY** Then leave, satisfied that you've done all you can, and let the child wake her with its crying. A ewe that does not respond to the baaing of its own lamb will never respond to the bleating of a calf.
VERGES 'Tis very true.	**VERGES** So true.
DOGBERRY This is the end of the charge:- you, constable, are to present the prince's own person: if you meet the prince in the night, you may stay him.	**DOGBERRY** So that's your job. You, constable, represent the prince himself. If you meet the prince in the night, you may order him to stop.
VERGES Nay, by'r our lady, that I think a' cannot.	**VERGES** No, by our Lady, I don't think he can do that.
DOGBERRY Five shillings to one on't, with any man that knows the statutes, he may stay him: marry, not without the prince be willing; for, indeed, the watch ought to offend no man; and it is an offence to stay a man against his will.	**DOGBERRY** I'll bet five shillings to one with any man that knows the law that he may order him to stop. Only if the Prince is willing to stop, of course, for the Watch should try not to offend anyone, and it is an offence to stop a man against his will.
VERGES By'r lady, I think it be so.	**VERGES** By our Lady, I think that's right.
DOGBERRY Ha, ha, ha! Well, masters, good night: an there be any matter of weight chances, call up me: keep your fellows' counsels and your own; and good night. Come, neighbour.	**DOGBERRY** Ha, ha, ha! Well, gentlemen, good night. If anything important happens, come and let me know. Keep each other's secrets, and your own. And so, good night! Come, friend.
Watchman Well, masters, we hear our charge: let us go sit here upon the church-bench till two, and then all to bed.	**Watchman** Well, gentlemen, we've heard what we have to do. Let's sit here on the church bench until two in the morning then go off to bed.
DOGBERRY One word more, honest neighbours. I pray you watch	**DOGBERRY** One thing more, good gentlemen. Please keep an eye on Sir Leonato's house: what with the wedding

about Signior Leonato's door; for the wedding being there to-morrow, there is a great coil to-night. Adieu: be vigitant, I beseech you.	there tomorrow, there's bound to be a great deal of coming and going. Goodbye, and be vigilant, I implore you.
Exeunt DOGBERRY and VERGES	*DOGBERRY and VERGES both exit.*
Enter BORACHIO and CONRADE	*BORACHIO and CONRADE enter*
BORACHIO What Conrade!	**BORACHIO** Conrade!
Watchman [Aside] Peace! stir not.	**Watchman** *(whispering)* Shh! Don't move
BORACHIO Conrade, I say!	**BORACHIO** Conrade, I say!
CONRADE Here, man; I am at thy elbow.	**CONRADE** I'm right here man, at your elbow.
BORACHIO Mass, and my elbow itched; I thought there would a scab follow.	**BORACHIO** By what's holy I felt my elbow itch - I thought I'd find a scab there!
CONRADE I will owe thee an answer for that: and now forward with thy tale.	**CONRADE** I'll get you back for that one later - now, get on with your story.
BORACHIO Stand thee close, then, under this pent-house, for it drizzles rain; and I will, like a true drunkard, utter all to thee.	**BORACHIO** Stand under this overhang with me as its starting to rain and, like a drunkard, I'll tell you everything.
Watchman [Aside] Some treason, masters: yet stand close.	**Watchman** *(quietly, to the other watchmen)* There's treachery afoot, men: remain hidden.
BORACHIO Therefore know I have earned of Don John a thousand ducats.	**BORACHIO** You should know I have earned a thousand gold pieces from Don John.
CONRADE Is it possible that any villany should be so dear?	**CONRADE** Is it possible that any crime could be so expensive?
BORACHIO Thou shouldst rather ask if it were possible any villany should be so rich; for when rich villains have need of poor ones, poor ones may make what price they will.	**BORACHIO** You should rather ask if it is possible that any crime could be worth so much; for when rich villains have need of poor ones, the poor ones can name their price
CONRADE I wonder at it.	**CONRADE** I am amazed.
BORACHIO That shows thou art unconfirmed. Thou knowest that	**BORACHIO** That shows how inexperienced you are. You know that the style of a jacket, or a hat, or a cloak tells you nothing about a man.

the fashion of a doublet, or a hat, or a cloak, is nothing to a man.	
CONRADE Yes, it is apparel.	**CONRADE** Yes, it's just clothing
BORACHIO I mean, the fashion.	**BORACHIO** I mean, the fashion.
CONRADE Yes, the fashion is the fashion.	**CONRADE** Yes, the fashion is the fashion.
BORACHIO Tush! I may as well say the fool's the fool. But seest thou not what a deformed thief this fashion is?	**BORACHIO** Oh for...! I may as well say the fool's the fool! But don't you see what a deformed thief fashion is - one who steals the truth by changing the appearance?
Watchman [Aside] I know that Deformed; a' has been a vile thief this seven year; a' goes up and down like a gentleman: I remember his name.	**Watchman** *(To himself)* I know that man Deformed - for the last seven years he's been a wicked thief. He walks about like a proper gentleman. I remember the name.
BORACHIO Didst thou not hear somebody?	**BORACHIO** Did you hear somebody?
CONRADE No; 'twas the vane on the house.	**CONRADE** No - it was the weathervane turning.
BORACHIO Seest thou not, I say, what a deformed thief this fashion is? how giddily a' turns about all the hot bloods between fourteen and five-and-thirty? sometimes fashioning them like Pharaoh's soldiers in the reeky painting, sometime like god Bel's priests in the old church-window, sometime like the shaven Hercules in the smirched worm-eaten tapestry, where his codpiece seems as massy as his club?	**BORACHIO** Do you understand what I'm saying about fashion stealing the truth about people? How all the hot-blooded young men are constantly changing their appearance? One day they look like Pharoah's army in that grimy painting, the next day like god Baal's priests in the stained glass window of the old church; another day they look like heroic Hercules in that grubby moth-eaten tapestry - the one where his codpiece is as big as his club!
CONRADE All this I see; and I see that the fashion wears out more apparel than the man. But art not thou thyself giddy with the fashion too, that thou hast shifted out of thy tale into telling me of the fashion?	**CONRADE** I can see that - and I also see more clothes are thrown away because they go out of fashion than because they wear out. But aren't you a bit fashion obsessed yourself? You've stopped mid-story and started talking about fashion instead!
BORACHIO Not so, neither: but know that I have to-night wooed Margaret, the Lady Hero's gentlewoman, by the name of Hero: she leans me out at her mistress' chamber-window, bids me a thousand times good night,--I tell this tale vilely:--I should first tell thee how the prince, Claudio and my master,	**BORACHIO** No, I'm not obsessed - but what I was going to tell you is this: this very night, I have wooed Margaret, Lady Hero's companion, all the while calling her 'Hero'. She was leaning out of Hero's bedroom window and wished me 'a thousand times good night' - but I'm telling the story badly: I should have told you first that my master Don John, had

planted and placed and possessed by my master Don John, saw afar off in the orchard this amiable encounter.	arranged for the Prince and Claudio to come with him to watch this amorous encounter from a way off in the orchard.
CONRADE And thought they Margaret was Hero?	**CONRADE** And they thought Margaret was Hero?
BORACHIO Two of them did, the prince and Claudio; but the devil my master knew she was Margaret; and partly by his oaths, which first possessed them, partly by the dark night, which did deceive them, but chiefly by my villany, which did confirm any slander that Don John had made, away went Claudio enraged; swore he would meet her, as he was appointed, next morning at the temple, and there, before the whole congregation, shame her with what he saw o'er night and send her home again without a husband.	**BORACHIO** The Prince and Claudio did, but that devil, my master knew it was Margaret. Partly because of my master's testimony, which first planted the idea in their minds; partly because of the darkness of the night; but mostly because of my villainous actions - which confirmed Don John's slanderous lies - Claudio left in a fury, swearing that he would turn up at the ceremony as planned and there, before the whole congregation, shame her by saying what he had seen in the night - and send her home husbandless.
First Watchman We charge you, in the prince's name, stand!	**First Watchman** We order you, in the Prince's name, don't move!
Second Watchman Call up the right master constable. We have here recovered the most dangerous piece of lechery that ever was known in the commonwealth.	**Second Watchman** Call for the Chief Constable, Dogberry. We have here recovered the most dangerous piece of lechery that has ever taken place in the commonwealth.
First Watchman And one Deformed is one of them: I know him; a' wears a lock.	**First Watchman** And one of them is Deformed: I recognise him - he wears a lovelock.
CONRADE Masters, masters,-	**CONRADE** Gentlemen, gentlemen -
Second Watchman You'll be made bring Deformed forth, I warrant you.	**Second Watchman** You'll be made to accompany Deformed , I assure you
CONRADE Masters,-	**CONRADE** Gentlemen,-
First Watchman Never speak: we charge you let us obey you to go with us.	**First Watchman** Don't speak: we obey you to go with us.
BORACHIO We are like to prove a goodly commodity, being taken up of these men's bills.	**BORACHIO** It seems we are a valuable commodity, for these men all carry bills*.
CONRADE A commodity in question, I warrant you. Come, we'll obey you.	**CONRADE** A commodity to be closely examined, I'll bet. Lead on - we'll obey you.

Exeunt	*All exit* bills* = weapons; receipts for good still to be paid for.

Analysis of Act 3 Scene 3

Two of the key stories have reached 'cliff-hanger' moments: Beatrice and Benedick have not yet met since their resolve to be open about their love and Claudio is about to see Hero disgraced. Shakespeare doesn't want to satisfy our curiosity just yet, so he brings in the sub-plot characters. These are the people the **groundlings** [poorer members of the audience who stood throughout the performance] would identify with, while the more educated, wealthier audience would enjoy laughing at their silliness.

Summary:
Dogberry, the Master Constable, and Verges, his Deputy, are appointing an extra constable to help keep watch on the night before the wedding. Dogberry thinks he is very clever, but though he tries to sound clever, he ends up talking nonsense. The watchmen ask him lots of questions about their duties and his advice is ridiculous – for example, he suggests they run away if they see a thief.

Despite being told that the best way they could keep watch is by sleeping, the watchmen are alert and realise that Borachio has been up to no good – in fact, the first watchman thinks he recognises him as a longstanding thief: we know that this is unlikely as Borachio has been in Don John's army.

The watchmen listen to Borachio tell Conrad how Margaret, wearing Hero's clothes and answering to her name was wooed by him at Hero's bedroom window, watched from the orchard – the same place where Benedick was tricked, by Claudio and Don Pedro. He claims they believed the hoax because firstly Don John had insinuated what they would see, secondly because it was a dark night and they couldn't see properly, but mostly because of the way he acted, confirming Don John's slander.

Having overheard all this, the watchmen arrest Borachio and Conrade, who, not really taking them seriously, go along without fuss.

Genre:
In this scene the comedy is more 'slapstick', relying on Dogberry and the watch having high opinions of their own cleverness while getting everything wrong.

Dogberry uses **malapropisms**: mistakenly replacing the right word [usually more sophisticated than required] with another that sounds similar, but has a completely different meaning. For example, Dogberry says 'suffer salvation' – being saved- when he means 'damnation' –having no hope of being saved.

Structure:
This scene is part of what is called the **sub-plot**, a story focusing on the lesser characters, but nonetheless impacting on the main story. Often is offers light relief and helps maintain pace, by diverting attention from the main story while time passes. Some critics complain that the sub-plot turns out to be more entertaining than the main plot, but the key thing is there's something for everyone in the Elizabethan audience.

Context:
There weren't policemen in Shakespeare's day; their duties were carried out by the Watch, who were so incompetent Elizabethan playwrights regularly mocked them as Shakespeare does here. And yet, they are the heroes of the play. Apparently, Dogberry and Verges were modelled on a real constable and deputy who lived in Grendon in Buckinghamshire, which is on Shakespeare's route from Stratford to London, a route used by many strolling players. The story is that they arrested

Shakespeare for sleeping on the porch of the parish church, claiming he'd stolen from the church. However, when they opened the chest they found nothing missing, to which Shakespeare apparently responded, 'Much ado about nothing'.
Elizabethan fashions also need some explaining: they really did distort – or 'deform'- the human figure with padding in some places and tight corsets to flatten others. Both males and females wore elaborately bejeweled costumes. Aristocratic men often wasted fortunes on dressing to outdo each other, wearing foreign fashions to show how international they were. They covered themselves in expensive perfume [as Benedick is accused of doing in the previous scene] and wore a lovelock of long hair over their shoulder. Some even wore makeup.

The working classes, however, were not even allowed to wear costly fabrics, never mind jewels. So Margaret would be breaking the law by impersonating Hero.

Themes:

- Appearance and reality

When Borachio seems to natter on about fashion, he is developing a metaphor begun at the start of the play when Beatrice says of Benedick: '... he wears his faith but as the fashion of his hat, it ever changes with the next block'. This suggests that though he may look respectable, he is actually unfaithful and disloyal. In the previous scene Benedick has been mocked for the way he dresses, trying to incorporate fashion's from other European countries in order to be at the forefront of fashion. This was something many of the young English nobility did, so Shakespeare is also teasing his audience when he has Claudio hint that love has made Benedick even more ridiculous.

Costumes for both genders were extremely ornate and expensive; people were actually forbidden by law to wear fabrics above their rank – only actors were allowed to on stage; Borachio extends this idea to the way rich Don John can buy any truth he likes to 'wear' or 'put on'. He gets slightly side-tracked into commenting about current fashions, seeming to suggest that Elizabethans change their fashions too easily; but the point he is getting to is that merely by wearing Hero's clothes and answering to her name, Margaret and he have – through appearance only – created a false reality, a 'deformed fashion' or look, that Claudio and Don Pedro will be acting on at the wedding.

Act 3 Scene 4

ORIGINAL TEXT	MODERN TRANSLATION
HERO's apartment.	**HERO's apartment.**
Enter HERO, MARGARET, and URSULA	*HERO, MARGARET, and URSULA enter*
HERO Good Ursula, wake my cousin Beatrice, and desire her to rise.	**HERO** Ursula, dear - wake my cousin Beatrice and ask her to get up.
URSULA I will, lady.	**URSULA** I will, my lady.
HERO And bid her come hither.	**HERO** And ask her to come here.
URSULA Well.	**URSULA** Very well.
Exit	*Ursula exits*
MARGARET Troth, I think your other rabato were better.	**MARGARET** Really, I think your other ruff is better.
HERO No, pray thee, good Meg, I'll wear this.	**HERO** No, please, dear Meg, I'll wear this one.
MARGARET By my troth, 's not so good; and I warrant your cousin will say so.	**MARGARET** I really think it's not as good; and I'm sure your cousin will agree with me.
HERO My cousin's a fool, and thou art another: I'll wear none but this.	**HERO** Well my cousin's a fool then - and you're another one: I'll wear this and none other.
MARGARET I like the new tire within excellently, if the hair were a thought browner; and your gown's a most rare fashion, i' faith. I saw the Duchess of Milan's gown that they praise so.	**MARGARET** I like the new head-dress and hair extensions very much, though the hair could perhaps be a touch browner - and your dress is really stylish. I saw the Duchess of Milan's dress - the one everybody praises.
HERO O, that exceeds, they say.	**HERO** Oh, they say that one surpasses all others.
MARGARET By my troth, 's but a night-gown in respect of yours: cloth o' gold, and cuts, and laced with silver, set with pearls, down sleeves, side sleeves, and skirts, round underborne with a bluish tinsel: but for a fine, quaint, graceful and excellent fashion, yours is worth ten on 't.	**MARGARET** I promise you that compared to yours, it's no better than a dressing gown. It has gold threads woven in, and fashionable slashes to show the fabric below, and it's trimmed with silver lace and embroidered with pearls. It has both full sleeves and ornamental sleeves, and the skirt is trimmed with sparkling metallic blue: but for elegance, grace and style, yours is ten times better.

HERO God give me joy to wear it! for my heart is exceeding heavy.	**HERO** I hope I enjoy wearing it! My heart is very heavy.
MARGARET 'Twill be heavier soon by the weight of a man.	**MARGARET** It will be even heavier soon - by the weight of a man.
HERO Fie upon thee! art not ashamed?	**HERO** What a thing to say! Have you no shame?
MARGARET Of what, lady? of speaking honourably? Is not marriage honourable in a beggar? Is not your lord honourable without marriage? I think you would have me say, 'saving your reverence, a husband:' and bad thinking do not wrest true speaking, I'll offend nobody: is there any harm in 'the heavier for a husband'? None, I think, and it be the right husband and the right wife; otherwise 'tis light, and not heavy: ask my Lady Beatrice else; here she comes.	**MARGARET** What should I be ashamed of, my lady? Sex within marriage is honourable, and isn't marriage honourable even for a beggar? And isn't your husband-to-be an honourable man? Must I now say 'Oh pardon me for using the word "husband"!'? If people don't twist my honest words with their own unworthy thoughts, nobody will be offended by what I say. What's wrong with saying 'heavier by the weight of a man'? Nothing, in my opinion, as long as it is the right husband and the right wife. Anything else might not be heavy, but it's not honourable either. You ask Lady Beatrice - here she is now.
Enter BEATRICE	*BEATRICE enters*
HERO Good morrow, coz.	**HERO** Good morning, cousin.
BEATRICE Good morrow, sweet Hero.	**BEATRICE** Good morning, sweet Hero.
HERO Why how now? do you speak in the sick tune?	**HERO** Are you OK? You sound out of sorts, your voice has a sad tune?
BEATRICE I am out of all other tune, methinks.	**BEATRICE** It is the only tune I have right now.
MARGARET Clap's into 'Light o' love;' that goes without a burden: do you sing it, and I'll dance it.	**MARGARET** Well if it's a tune we want, how about 'Light of Love.' It requires no male voice. You sing it, and I'll dance to it.
BEATRICE Ye light o' love, with your heels! then, if your husband have stables enough, you'll see he shall lack no barns.	**BEATRICE** Well you're certainly on your heels where men are concerned! You'll have no shortage of children if your husband has enough stables for you to roll in the hay out of his sight!
MARGARET O illegitimate construction! I scorn that with my heels.	**MARGARET** It's your interpretation that's illegitimate, not the children I might have! I kick it away with my heels.

BEATRICE 'Tis almost five o'clock, cousin; tis time you were ready. By my troth, I am exceeding ill: heigh-ho!	**BEATRICE** It's almost five o'clock, cousin. It's time you were ready. I really do feel out of sorts. Ah well!
MARGARET For a hawk, a horse, or a husband?	**MARGARET** Are you sighing for a hawk, a horse, or a husband?
BEATRICE For the letter that begins them all, H.	**BEATRICE** They all begin with at H - well, I sigh because I ache.
MARGARET Well, and you be not turned Turk, there's no more sailing by the star.	**MARGARET** Well, if you haven't changed your views on marriage, I don't know what to believe any more.
BEATRICE What means the fool, trow?	**BEATRICE** What does the fool mean by that, do you suppose?
MARGARET Nothing I; but God send every one their heart's desire!	**MARGARET** I mean nothing by it - but God sends everyone their heart's desire!
HERO These gloves the count sent me; they are an excellent perfume.	**HERO** These gloves the Count sent me are beautifully perfumed.
BEATRICE I am stuffed, cousin; I cannot smell.	**BEATRICE** I'm all stuffed up, cousin. I can't smell a thing
MARGARET A maid, and stuffed! there's goodly catching of cold.	**MARGARET** An unmarried woman - and stuffed! That's what I call catching a cold!
BEATRICE O, God help me! God help me! how long have you professed apprehension?	**BEATRICE** Oh, God help me! God help me! How long have you been the great wit?
MARGARET Even since you left it. Doth not my wit become me rarely?	**MARGARET** Even since you stopped. Don't you think my wit suits me?
BEATRICE It is not seen enough, you should wear it in your cap. By my troth, I am sick.	**BEATRICE** We don't see enough of it - you should wear it as a feather in your cap. I really do feel unwell.
MARGARET Get you some of this distilled Carduus Benedictus, and lay it to your heart: it is the only thing for a qualm.	**MARGARET** Take some of this distilled Carduus Benedictus - Holy Thistle, and put it on your chest: it's the only thing for nausea and faintness.
HERO There thou prickest her with a thistle.	**HERO** I think you've managed to prick her with that thistle.
BEATRICE Benedictus! why Benedictus? you have some moral in this Benedictus.	**BEATRICE** Benedictus! why Benedictus? Are you suggesting a double meaning in Benedictus?

MARGARET Moral! no, by my troth, I have no moral meaning; I meant, plain holy-thistle. You may think perchance that I think you are in love: nay, by'r lady, I am not such a fool to think what I list, nor I list not to think what I can, nor indeed I cannot think, if I would think my heart out of thinking, that you are in love or that you will be in love or that you can be in love. Yet Benedick was such another, and now is he become a man: he swore he would never marry, and yet now, in despite of his heart, he eats his meat without grudging: and how you may be converted I know not, but methinks you look with your eyes as other women do.	**MARGARET** Double-meaning! Goodness me no! There's no hidden meaning; I just meant plain old Holy Thistle. Do you perhaps think that I think that you're in love? By our Lady no! I am not such a fool as to think whatever I like, and I don't like to think what I can or can't think, even if I could think my heart right out of thinking, that you are in love or that you will be in love or that you can be in love. Yet Benedick was like that once, and now he has totally grown up: he swore he would never get married and yet now he happily eats his words and loves ungrudgingly. What it will take to change you, I've no idea, but I think that you notice things just like other women do.
BEATRICE What pace is this that thy tongue keeps?	**BEATRICE** What do you call this pace that your tongue is running at?
MARGARET Not a false gallop.	**MARGARET** It's running at a gallop, but it's not put on.
Re-enter URSULA	*Re-enter URSULA*
URSULA Madam, withdraw: the prince, the count, Signior Benedick, Don John, and all the gallants of the town, are come to fetch you to church.	**URSULA** Madam, we have to go: the Prince, the Count, Sir Benedick, Don John, and all the fine gentlemen of the town have come to take you to the church.
HERO Help to dress me, good coz, good Meg, good Ursula.	**HERO** Help to get dressed good cousin, good Meg, good Ursula.
Exeunt	*They all exit*

Analysis of Act 3 scene 4

This is the companion scene to Act 3 scene 2: the focus is on fashion and being teased about love, but whereas the men were lively, the ladies are strangely subdued.

Summary:
On the morning of the wedding Hero send Ursula to wake Beatrice, while Margaret helps her to dress. Margaret gossips about fashion and then makes a joke about sex. Hero isn't really in the mood and complains that she feels apprehensive – heavy hearted, as though anticipating something will go wrong. When Beatrice joins them it is clear she's no bundle of joy either – she apparently has a cold, though it might be that she has spent the night crying. When she insists that she is ill, she's offered medicine called 'Carduus benedictus', the Latin name for a popular cure-all known as 'Holy Thistle'. Of course she immediately suspects they're teasing her about Benedick. Margaret is the only excited one: perhaps because of her night with Borachio. She chatters and teases in contrast to the subdued Hero and the gloomy Beatrice. When Ursula enters she hurries them up with news that the men have arrived to escort Hero to church.

Genre:
A classic definition of comedy is that at least one couple get to live happily ever after in married bliss; Shakespeare plays with this idea by getting the wedding day of the ideal couple off to a dull start – there's no 'fairytale' quality about Hero's exceedingly heavy heart and Beatrice's sniffles.

Structure:
This scene is the counterpart to Benedick's being teased about his sudden interest in fashion and love for Beatrice, but it is Hero and Margaret who discuss fashion and Margaret who teases Beatrice about Benedick. Benedick had 'toothache', Beatrice has a 'cold'. Margaret is completely innocent of the plot to disgrace Hero.

Language:
There is a lot of sexual innuendo in this scene, perhaps a reminder of Margaret's night of wooing and to show the contrast between her ebullience [jollity/cheerfulness] and the bride Hero's 'heaviness' or depression, and Beatrice's sadness. A word like 'stuffed' refers both to a 'blocked nose' and to being pregnant. The song 'Light of Love' was a popular dance song in Shakespeare's day and though the words have been lost, the music still exists. But Shakespeare mentions it because carries on the joke of being 'heavier for a husband' as 'light' can mean 'immoral'. Margaret says, it goes without a burden', meaning the 'weight' of the male voices – bass- is missing. In her reply Beatrice shows she understands this, because 'kicking up your heels' could refer to sexual immorality, while 'barns' puns on 'bairns' or children. While it isn't important to understand the puns, it is important to see that Margaret is playing the part of wit Beatrice usually fulfills – so much so that Beatrice suggests she wears it like a feather in her cap – and is buoyed up, while the two ladies are depressed.

Act 3 Scene 5

ORIGINAL TEXT	MODERN TRANSLATION
Another room in LEONATO'S house.	**Another room in LEONATO'S house.**
Enter LEONATO, with DOGBERRY and VERGES	*LEONATO enters with DOGBERRY and VERGES*
LEONATO What would you with me, honest neighbour?	**LEONATO** What do you want with me, my good fellow?
DOGBERRY Marry, sir, I would have some confidence with you that decerns you nearly.	**DOGBERRY** Well, Sir, I would like to confide with you about a matter that *discerns* you closely.
LEONATO Brief, I pray you; for you see it is a busy time with me.	**LEONATO** Be brief, please: you can see this is a busy time for me.
DOGBERRY Marry, this it is, sir.	**DOGBERRY** Indeed it is, sir.
VERGES Yes, in truth it is, sir.	**VERGES** Yes it truly is, sir.
LEONATO What is it, my good friends?	**LEONATO** What is it, my good friends?
DOGBERRY Goodman Verges, sir, speaks a little off the matter: an old man, sir, and his wits are not so blunt as, God help, I would desire they were; but, in faith, honest as the skin between his brows.	**DOGBERRY** The good yeoman Verges, sir, tends to ramble. He's getting on a bit, sir, and, God help him, his wits are not as blunt as I would like them to be - but he is as honest as the skin between his brows.
VERGES Yes, I thank God I am as honest as any man living that is an old man and no honester than I.	**VERGES** Yes, I thank God that I am as honest as all the other old men who are no more honest than me.
DOGBERRY Comparisons are odorous: *palabras*, neighbour Verges.	**DOGBERRY** Comparisons are odorous: *'Few words!'* on with your story, comrade Verges.
LEONATO Neighbours, you are tedious.	**LEONATO** Friends, you are tedious.
DOGBERRY It pleases your worship to say so, but we are the poor duke's officers; but truly, for mine own part, if I were as tedious as a king, I could find it in my heart to bestow it all of your worship.	**DOGBERRY** Your worship may say that, but we're just the poor duke's officers. But for myself, if I was as tedious as a king, I would give it all to you your worship.
LEONATO All thy tediousness on me, ah?	**LEONATO** All your tediousness for me, eh?

DOGBERRY Yea, an 'twere a thousand pound more than 'tis; for I hear as good exclamation on your worship as of any man in the city; and though I be but a poor man, I am glad to hear it.	**DOGBERRY** Indeed - even if it was a thousand pound more than it is, I still would, for I hear you are exclaimed in this city, and though I am only a poor man, I am glad to hear such things.
VERGES And so am I.	**VERGES** And so am I.
LEONATO I would fain know what you have to say.	**LEONATO** I would be very glad to know what you have to say.
VERGES Marry, sir, our watch to-night, excepting your worship's presence, ha' ta'en a couple of as arrant knaves as any in Messina.	**VERGES** Very good, sir, our watch tonight, *excepting* your worship's presence, has caught two of the worst villains in Messina.
DOGBERRY A good old man, sir; he will be talking: as they say, when the age is in, the wit is out: God help us! it is a world to see. Well said, i' faith, neighbour Verges: well, God's a good man; an two men ride of a horse, one must ride behind. An honest soul, i' faith, sir; by my troth he is, as ever broke bread; but God is to be worshipped; all men are not alike; alas, good neighbour!	**DOGBERRY** He's a good old man, sir, but he does go on a bit - as the saying goes, 'when the age is in, the wit is out'. God help us, what a world! You said it right, indeed you did, comrade Verges. Well, God's a just man, and if two men ride on one horse, one must sit behind the other. Verges is as honest a man as any that's lived, but God in his wisdom did not create all men the same. It is a shame, my friend!
LEONATO Indeed, neighbour, he comes too short of you.	**LEONATO** Indeed, friend, he doesn't speak at such great length as you.
DOGBERRY Gifts that God gives.	**DOGBERRY** God gives us all different gifts.
LEONATO I must leave you.	**LEONATO** I must leave you now.
DOGBERRY One word, sir: our watch, sir, have indeed comprehended two aspicious persons, and we would have them this morning examined before your worship.	**DOGBERRY** Before you go, sir: our watch, sir, has indeed *comprehended* two *auspicious* people, and we would like them to be examined by your worship this morning.
LEONATO Take their examination yourself and bring it me: I am now in great haste, as it may appear unto you.	**LEONATO** Examine them yourself and bring me your findings. As you can see, I'm in a great hurry.
DOGBERRY It shall be suffigance.	**DOGBERRY** That will be *suffigance*.
LEONATO Drink some wine ere you go: fare you well. *Enter a Messenger*	**LEONATO** Have some wine to drink before you leave. Go well! *A Messenger enters*

Original	Modern
Messenger My lord, they stay for you to give your daughter to her husband.	**Messenger** My lord, they're waiting for you to give your daughter away to Claudio.
LEONATO I'll wait upon them: I am ready.	**LEONATO** I'll be right there..
Exeunt LEONATO and Messenger	*LEONATO and the Messenger both exit.*
DOGBERRY Go, good partner, go, get you to Francis Seacole; bid him bring his pen and inkhorn to the gaol: we are now to examination these men.	**DOGBERRY** Go, good fellow, and find Francis Seacole: tell him to bring his pen and ink to the jail - we must now go to *examination* these men.
VERGES And we must do it wisely.	**VERGES** And we must do it wisely.
DOGBERRY We will spare for no wit, I warrant you; here's that shall drive some of them to a non-come: only get the learned writer to set down our excommunication and meet me at the gaol.	**DOGBERRY** I guarantee we'll use the utmost cleverness. That will leave them totally *non-comed*. Now go and get that learned writer to record our *excommunication*, then meet me at the jail.
Exeunt	*Both exit*

Analysis of Act 3 Scene 5

Here is dramatic irony at its most powerful to create tension in a scene that is also very funny and played for laughs. The audience knows how important it is for Leonato to hear the news before the wedding, but Dogberry and Verges just don't get to the point and the opportunity to save Hero humiliation is lost.

Summary:
Dogberry and Verges want Leonato to be present when they examine Borachio and Conrade, but they take so long getting to the point and their malapropisms make what they say incomprehensible at the very time when Leonato is rushing to prepare for the wedding. So he tells them to question the men without him, then let him know what they find. He is called to give Hero away and rushes off, while they make arrangements to meet at the jail for the examination.

Structure:
This scene forms a 'pair' with Act 3 scene 3 because it also features Dogberry and Verges, relies on malapropisms for humour and creates tension by slowing the action down just as the audience is eager to find out what happens next.

Context:
Dogberry and Verges have become some of Shakespeare's most loved double acts. In this play they also form a counterpart to the witty sparring of Beatrice in Benedick. Perhaps this popularity is due in some part to William Kemp, a famous Elizabethan comedian. In the 1623 'First folio' edition of the play his name is sometimes written instead of Dogberry's, indicating that he played the role. Shakespeare created many comic roles specifically for Kemp to play, like that of 'Bottom' in *A Midsummer Night's Dream.*

Language:
Although you can get the general idea without knowing exactly which words Dogberry has wrong, it is more amusing when you can recognise his malapropisms and mangled sayings. Here are some of them:

Decerns [discerns] – **concerns;** 'blunt' should be **sharp;** odorous [having an odour/stink – **odious** [horrible]

'Tedious' means 'boring or monotonous', but Dogberry seems to think it means 'wealthy'!

exclamation [shout] – **acclamation** [enthusiastic approval] ; 'excepting excluding] your presence' should be **respecting your presence**, a set phrase apology for having to say something rude.

Comprehended [understood] – **apprehended** [arrested] ; 'aspicious', mispronunciation of 'auspicious' [fortunate] – **suspicious** [mistrustful]; 'suffigance' mispronunciation of **sufficient**

Act 4 Scene 1

ORIGINAL TEXT	MODERN TRANSLATION
A church.	**A church.**
Enter DON PEDRO, DON JOHN, LEONATO, FRIAR FRANCIS, CLAUDIO, BENEDICK, HERO, BEATRICE, and Attendants	*Enter DON PEDRO, DON JOHN, LEONATO, FRIAR FRANCIS, CLAUDIO, BENEDICK, HERO, BEATRICE, and Attendants*
LEONATO Come, Friar Francis, be brief; only to the plain form of marriage, and you shall recount their particular duties afterwards.	**LEONATO** Come, Friar Francis, be quick; stick to the basic marriage service - you can explain the finer details of who promises what afterwards.
FRIAR FRANCIS You come hither, my lord, to marry this lady.	**FRIAR FRANCIS** *starting the service* You come here, my lord, to marry this lady.
CLAUDIO No.	**CLAUDIO** No.
LEONATO To be married to her: friar, you come to marry her.	**LEONATO** To be married to her: Friar, *you* come to marry her.
FRIAR FRANCIS Lady, you come hither to be married to this count.	**FRIAR FRANCIS** Lady, you come here to be married to this count.
HERO I do.	**HERO** I do.
FRIAR FRANCIS If either of you know any inward impediment why you should not be conjoined, I charge you, on your souls, to utter it.	**FRIAR FRANCIS** If either of you know any reason why you should not be joined in marriage, you must mention it now, for your soul's sake.
CLAUDIO Know you any, Hero?	**CLAUDIO** Do you know any, Hero?
HERO None, my lord.	**HERO** None, my lord.
FRIAR FRANCIS Know you any, count?	**FRIAR FRANCIS** Do you know any, Claudio?
LEONATO I dare make his answer, none.	**LEONATO** I dare to answer on his behalf: none.
CLAUDIO O, what men dare do! what men may do! what men daily do, not knowing what they do!	**CLAUDIO** O, what men dare do! what men may do! what men do everyday, not knowing what they do!
BENEDICK How now! interjections? Why, then, some be of laughing, as, ah, ha, he!	**BENEDICK** Good grief! interjections? I suppose they must be joking: ah, ha, he!

CLAUDIO Stand thee by, friar. Father, by your leave: Will you with free and unconstrained soul Give me this maid, your daughter?	**CLAUDIO** Hold on a minute, friar. Father Leonato, with your permission: Will you, without a guilty conscience Give me this virgin, your daughter?
LEONATO As freely, son, as God did give her me.	**LEONATO** As freely, son, as God gave her to me.
CLAUDIO And what have I to give you back, whose worth May counterpoise this rich and precious gift?	**CLAUDIO** And what have I got to give you that is worth as much as this rich and precious gift?
DON PEDRO Nothing, unless you render her again.	**DON PEDRO** Nothing, unless you give her back again.
CLAUDIO Sweet prince, you learn me noble thankfulness. There, Leonato, take her back again: Give not this rotten orange to your friend; She's but the sign and semblance of her honour. Behold how like a maid she blushes here! O, what authority and show of truth Can cunning sin cover itself withal! Comes not that blood as modest evidence To witness simple virtue? Would you not swear, All you that see her, that she were a maid, By these exterior shows? But she is none: She knows the heat of a luxurious bed; Her blush is guiltiness, not modesty.	**CLAUDIO** Sweet prince, you teach me the decent way to show my thankfulness. There, Leonato, take her back again: Don't give this rotten orange to your friend; She's a fake 'virgin', she only seems respectable. Look how she blushes as if she's innocent! Oh, sin is so cunning it disguises itself with signs we usually take as proof of innocence, like blushing. Doesn't that rush of blood we see seem to suggest that she's pure? Wouldn't you all, seeing her, swear, that she must be a virgin, by these outward signs? But she is not: she's hot stuff in bed; Her blush is guiltiness, not shy innocence.
LEONATO What do you mean, my lord?	**LEONATO** What do you mean, my lord Claudio?
CLAUDIO Not to be married, Not to knit my soul to an approved wanton.	**CLAUDIO** That I intend not to get married, Not to join my soul to a proven slut.
LEONATO Dear my lord, if you, in your own proof, Have vanquish'd the resistance of her youth, And made defeat of her virginity,--	**LEONATO** Good grief, Claudio, if you were unable to wait till the wedding, went too far and proved irresistible to this young virgin-
CLAUDIO I know what you would say: if I have known her, You will say she did embrace me as a husband, And so extenuate the 'forehand sin: No, Leonato, I never tempted her with word too large; But, as a brother to his sister, show'd Bashful sincerity and comely love.	**CLAUDIO** I know what you're trying to say: if I have had sex with her, you'll say she embraced me as a husband, And so excuse her 'jumping the gun': No, Leonato, I never tempted her with big promises or suggestive language; actually I treated her as a shy and sincere brother would show love to a sister.
HERO And seem'd I ever otherwise to you?	**HERO** And did I ever seem otherwise to you?
CLAUDIO Out on thee! Seeming! I will write against it: You seem to me as Dian in her orb,	**CLAUDIO** Away with you! Two faced! I will expose it publicly: You seem to me like Diana, the goddess of chastity

As chaste as is the bud ere it be blown; But you are more intemperate in your blood Than Venus, or those pamper'd animals That rage in savage sensuality.	and the moon, as unspoilt as is a rose bud before it loses any petals; But you are more excessively passionate than the goddess of love, Venus, or those spoilt animals who spend all their time having sex.
HERO Is my lord well, that he doth speak so wide?	**HERO** Are you sick, my lord?!How can you make these ridiculously untrue claims?
LEONATO Sweet prince, why speak not you?	**LEONATO** Please Don Pedro, why don't you say something?
DON PEDRO What should I speak? I stand dishonour'd, that have gone about To link my dear friend to a common stale.	**DON PEDRO** What should I say? I'm ashamed that I worked to arrange this marriage, linking my dear friend to a cheap prostitute.
LEONATO Are these things spoken, or do I but dream?	**LEONATO** Are these things actually being said, or am I dreaming?
DON JOHN Sir, they are spoken, and these things are true.	**DON JOHN** Sir, they are spoken, and these things are true.
BENEDICK This looks not like a nuptial.	**BENEDICK** *to no one in particular* This doesn't sound like a wedding.
HERO True! O God!	**HERO** True! Oh God!
CLAUDIO Leonato, stand I here? Is this the prince? is this the prince's brother? Is this face Hero's? are our eyes our own?	**CLAUDIO** Leonato, am I standing here? Is this the prince? is this the prince's brother? Is this face Hero's? are our eyes our own?
LEONATO All this is so: but what of this, my lord?	**LEONATO** Yes, that's so, but what do you mean by it my lord?
CLAUDIO Let me but move one question to your daughter; And, by that fatherly and kindly power That you have in her, bid her answer truly.	**CLAUDIO** Let me just put one question to your daughter; And, by that fatherly and kindly power That you have in her, ask her to answer truly.
LEONATO I charge thee do so, as thou art my child.	**LEONATO** *to Hero* I order you to do so, as you are my child.
HERO O, God defend me! how am I beset! What kind of catechising call you this?	**HERO** O, God defend me! Why am I under attack! What kind of cross-examination is this?
CLAUDIO To make you answer truly to your name.	**CLAUDIO** To make you answer truly to your legendary name.
HERO Is it not Hero? Who can blot that name With any just reproach?	**HERO** Is it not Hero, who was faithful in love? Who can claim with any truth that I've been less faithful?

CLAUDIO Marry, that can Hero; Hero itself can blot out Hero's virtue. What man was he talk'd with you yesternight Out at your window betwixt twelve and one? Now, if you are a maid, answer to this.	**CLAUDIO** Well, the legendary Hero can; The word 'Hero'*can blot out Hero's virtue. Who was the man talking with you last night outside your window between twelve and one? Now, if you are a virgin, explain that. *(spoken by Borachio)
HERO I talk'd with no man at that hour, my lord.	**HERO** I didn't speak to any man at that hour, my lord.
DON PEDRO Why, then are you no maiden. Leonato, I am sorry you must hear: upon mine honour, Myself, my brother and this grieved count Did see her, hear her, at that hour last night Talk with a ruffian at her chamber-window Who hath indeed, most like a liberal villain, Confess'd the vile encounters they have had A thousand times in secret.	**DON PEDRO** Why, then are you not a virgin. Leonato, I am sorry you must hear this: this is the truth, Myself, my brother and this wronged count, Claudio Saw her, heard her, at that hour last night Talk to a lout at her bedroom-window Who has actually confessed in course detail the despicable rendezvous they have had A thousand times in secret.
DON JOHN Fie, fie! they are not to be named, my lord, Not to be spoke of; There is not chastity enough in language Without offence to utter them. Thus, pretty lady, I am sorry for thy much misgovernment.	**DON JOHN** Stop! Stop! Don't go into details, my lord, Don't speak of them; Language is not pure enough to mention them without causing offence. *To Hero:* So, pretty lady, I regret your terrible misconduct.
CLAUDIO O Hero, what a Hero hadst thou been, If half thy outward graces had been placed About thy thoughts and counsels of thy heart! But fare thee well, most foul, most fair! farewell, Thou pure impiety and impious purity! For thee I'll lock up all the gates of love, And on my eyelids shall conjecture hang, To turn all beauty into thoughts of harm, And never shall it more be gracious.	**CLAUDIO** Oh Hero, what a Hero you could have been, If half your physical attractiveness had been reflected as virtues in your thoughts and your heart! But fare you well, most foul, most fair! goodbye, You pure immorality and sinful purity! For you I'll lock up all the gates of love, And I'll always be suspicious of attractive women, all beauty will remind me of this injury; beauty will never attract me again.
LEONATO Hath no man's dagger here a point for me? *HERO swoons*	**LEONATO** Has no man got a dagger I can kill myself with? *HERO faints*
BEATRICE Why, how now, cousin! wherefore sink you down?	**BEATRICE** What's the matter, cousin! Why are you falling down?
DON JOHN Come, let us go. These things, come thus to light, Smother her spirits up. *Exeunt DON PEDRO, DON JOHN, and CLAUDIO*	**DON JOHN** Come, let us go. The way these secret things have now been exposed, suffocates her spirit. *All exit DON PEDRO, DON JOHN, and CLAUDIO*
BENEDICK How doth the lady?	**BENEDICK** How is Hero?

BEATRICE Dead, I think. Help, uncle! Hero! why, Hero! Uncle! Signior Benedick! Friar!	**BEATRICE** Dead, I think. Help, uncle! Hero! why, Hero! Uncle! Sir Benedick! Friar!
LEONATO O Fate! take not away thy heavy hand. Death is the fairest cover for her shame That may be wish'd for.	**LEONATO** Oh Fate! Keep your heavy hand smothering her. Death is the best cover for her shame That we could wish for.
BEATRICE How now, cousin Hero!	**BEATRICE** Are you alright, cousin Hero!
FRIAR FRANCIS Have comfort, lady.	**FRIAR FRANCIS** Have comfort, lady.
LEONATO Dost thou look up?	**LEONATO** Do you dare look up?
FRIAR FRANCIS Yea, wherefore should she not?	**FRIAR FRANCIS** Yes, why shouldn't she look up to Heaven?
LEONATO Wherefore! Why, doth not every earthly thing Cry shame upon her? Could she here deny The story that is printed in her blood? Do not live, Hero; do not ope thine eyes: For, did I think thou wouldst not quickly die, Thought I thy spirits were stronger than thy shames, Myself would, on the rearward of reproaches, Strike at thy life. Grieved I, I had but one? Chid I for that at frugal nature's frame? O, one too much by thee! Why had I one? Why ever wast thou lovely in my eyes? Why had I not with charitable hand Took up a beggar's issue at my gates, Who smirch'd thus and mired with infamy, I might have said 'No part of it is mine; This shame derives itself from unknown loins'? But mine and mine I loved and mine I praised And mine that I was proud on, mine so much That I myself was to myself not mine, Valuing of her,--why, she, O, she is fallen Into a pit of ink, that the wide sea Hath drops too few to wash her clean again And salt too little which may season give To her foul-tainted flesh!	**LEONATO** Why not?! After all, doesn't everyone condemn her? Could she here deny the accusations when her blushes are evidence they're true? Do not live, Hero; do not open your eyes: because, if I thought you wouldn't die quickly, or that your will to live was stronger than your shame I would kill you myself. Was I ever sorry I only had one child? Did I ever blame nature for being so mean to me? Oh, one child like you is one too many! Why did I even have one child? Why were you ever lovely to my eyes? Why didn't I rather adopt a beggar's child at my gates, whose shame and dishonour I could now have denied, saying 'No part of this behaviour reflects on me; This shame originates from unknown parentage'? But you are mine and because you were mine I loved you and I praised you as mine. And because you were mine that I was proud of, I was also proud of how much you were like me. I actually thought less of myself and more of her, valuing her above all,--why, now she, Oh, she is fallen into a ditch of staining ink, that even the wide sea hasn't enough water to wash her clean again nor enough salt to cover her so that her rotten flesh could have been preserved as pure!
BENEDICK Sir, sir, be patient. For my part, I am so attired in wonder, I know not what to say.	**BENEDICK** Sir, sir, be patient. As far as I'm concerned, this is so unbelievable, I don't know what to say.
BEATRICE O, on my soul, my cousin is belied!	**BEATRICE** O, I'm sure my cousin has been falsely accused!

BENEDICK Lady, were you her bedfellow last night?	**BENEDICK** Lady, did you share her bedroom last night?
BEATRICE No, truly not; although, until last night, I have this twelvemonth been her bedfellow.	**BEATRICE** No, actually not; although, until last night, I had shared her room all year.
LEONATO Confirm'd, confirm'd! O, that is stronger made Which was before barr'd up with ribs of iron! Would the two princes lie, and Claudio lie, Who loved her so, that, speaking of her foulness, Wash'd it with tears? Hence from her! let her die.	**LEONATO** Confirmed, confirmed! Oh, that makes the strong evidence against Hero even more obviously true, as if iron bars were strengthened! Would the two princes, Don Pedro and Don John, lie, and Claudio – who loved her so much he was crying as he accused her- lie? Get away from her! let her die.
FRIAR FRANCIS Hear me a little; For I have only been silent so long And given way unto this course of fortune. By noting of the lady I have mark'd A thousand blushing apparitions To start into her face, a thousand innocent shames In angel whiteness beat away those blushes; And in her eye there hath appear'd a fire, To burn the errors that these princes hold Against her maiden truth. Call me a fool; Trust not my reading nor my observations, Which with experimental seal doth warrant The tenor of my book; trust not my age, My reverence, calling, nor divinity, If this sweet lady lie not guiltless here Under some biting error.	**FRIAR FRANCIS** Listen to me for a moment; I have only kept quiet so long to mull over this and think about what can be done. Observing Hero I've noticed how genuine her reactions have been, blushing with shame, turning pale with horror, yet also in her eyes a fire of determination to prove that the lies spoken by these princes are false, that she *is* pure… Call me a fool; Don't trust not my interpretation of my observations, Which are based on years of experience; don't trust my age, my reputation, my holiness, If this sweet lady, Hero, is not guiltless, lying here degraded by a painful and damaging mistake. I'm prepared to stake my reputation on it.
LEONATO Friar, it cannot be. Thou seest that all the grace that she hath left Is that she will not add to her damnation A sin of perjury; she not denies it: Why seek'st thou then to cover with excuse That which appears in proper nakedness?	**LEONATO** Friar, it can't be true. You can see that the only virtue she has left is that she won't damn herself even more by denying these accusations: why are you trying to cover the sin that has rightfully been exposed with excuses? Surely sin should be exposed as the naked truth?
FRIAR FRANCIS Lady, what man is he you are accused of?	**FRIAR FRANCIS** *ignoring Leonato* Lady, who is man you are accused of seeing?
HERO They know that do accuse me; I know none: If I know more of any man alive Than that which maiden modesty doth warrant, Let all my sins lack mercy! O my father, Prove you that any man with me conversed At hours unmeet, or that I yesternight Maintain'd the change of words with any creature, Refuse me, hate me, torture me to death!	**HERO** I have no idea – my accusers know who they mean: If I have a more intimate knowledge of any man alive than a decent virgin ought to have, Let none of my sins be forgiven! Oh my father, If you can prove that any man chatted with me At unsociable times, or that I even exchanged words with any creature last night, Refuse to know me, hate me, torture me to death!
FRIAR FRANCIS There is some strange misprision in the princes.	**FRIAR FRANCIS** The princes are under some strange misconception.

BENEDICK Two of them have the very bent of honour; And if their wisdoms be misled in this, The practise of it lives in John the bastard, Whose spirits toil in frame of villanies.	**BENEDICK** Two of are absolutely honourable men; So if they've misunderstood anything in this, John the bastard, who uses every opportunity to be a villain, is certainly to blame.
LEONATO I know not. If they speak but truth of her, These hands shall tear her; if they wrong her honour, The proudest of them shall well hear of it. Time hath not yet so dried this blood of mine, Nor age so eat up my invention, Nor fortune made such havoc of my means, Nor my bad life reft me so much of friends, But they shall find, awaked in such a kind, Both strength of limb and policy of mind, Ability in means and choice of friends, To quit me of them throughly.	**LEONATO** Well, I'm not sure. If they're telling the truth about her, these hands of mine will tear her apart; but if they're slandering her honour, even the most important of them better beware – I'm not so old that I won't seek revenge nor so poor that I'm powerless, nor am I without friends I can rely on to support me ; whether I get them back through physical strength, through strategy, or money and choice of friends, I will get rid of them completely.
FRIAR FRANCIS Pause awhile, And let my counsel sway you in this case. Your daughter here the princes left for dead: Let her awhile be secretly kept in, And publish it that she is dead indeed; Maintain a mourning ostentation And on your family's old monument Hang mournful epitaphs and do all rites That appertain unto a burial.	**FRIAR FRANCIS** Slow down! Let me advise you in this case. The princes left your daughter here for dead when she fainted: let her hide away secretly, but spread the word that she is really dead. Make a show of mourning her and on your family's old mausoleum hang sad verses and do all ritual things as if she really has been buried.
LEONATO What shall become of this? what will this do?	**LEONATO** What's the point? How will this change things?
FRIAR FRANCIS Marry, this well carried shall on her behalf Change slander to remorse; that is some good: But not for that dream I on this strange course, But on this travail look for greater birth. She dying, as it must so be maintain'd, Upon the instant that she was accused, Shall be lamented, pitied and excused Of every hearer: for it so falls out That what we have we prize not to the worth Whiles we enjoy it, but being lack'd and lost, Why, then we rack the value, then we find The virtue that possession would not show us Whiles it was ours. So will it fare with Claudio: When he shall hear she died upon his words, The idea of her life shall sweetly creep Into his study of imagination, And every lovely organ of her life Shall come apparell'd in more precious habit, More moving-delicate and full of life, Into the eye and prospect of his soul, Than when she lived indeed; then shall he mourn, If ever love had interest in his liver,	**FRIAR FRANCIS** Well, if we do this convincingly, slander will change to sorrow; that will do some good for a start: But that's not the main thing; I'm aiming higher: Because she died – as we're pretending - at the very moment that she was accused, she'll be lamented, pitied and excused by everyone who hears of it: the truth is, we never appreciate what we have till it is gone and then we value it even more than its real worth, seeing all sorts of worth in it. That will happen to Claudio: When he hears she died on hearing his accusation, He will begin to remember all the things he loved about her, he'll think about her all the time and every thought will dress her in more precious clothes. He'll love her even more than he did when she was alive and so really mourn her loss. Even if he still thought his accusation were the truth, he would be so full of love for her that he would wish he'd never confronted her with it. Let us follow this strategy, never doubting our eventual success so that the actual effect will be even more convincing than I envisage.

And wish he had not so accused her, No, though he thought his accusation true. Let this be so, and doubt not but success Will fashion the event in better shape Than I can lay it down in likelihood. But if all aim but this be levell'd false, The supposition of the lady's death Will quench the wonder of her infamy: And if it sort not well, you may conceal her, As best befits her wounded reputation, In some reclusive and religious life, Out of all eyes, tongues, minds and injuries.	But even if things don't work out like this, At least Hero's death will stop the rumours of her supposed unfaithfulness. As a last resort, if all our efforts fail, at least then she can be sent to a nunnery, the best place to hide someone with a bad reputation from all eyes, tongues, minds and gossip.
BENEDICK Signior Leonato, let the Friar advise you: And though you know my inwardness and love Is very much unto the prince and Claudio, Yet, by mine honour, I will deal in this As secretly and justly as your soul Should with your body.	**BENEDICK** Sir Leonato, let the Friar advise you: And though you know my friendship and loyalty are to the prince and Claudio, I promise, on my word of honour, to keep this an absolute secret.
LEONATO Being that I flow in grief, The smallest twine may lead me.	**LEONATO** Because I'm so upset, I'll hold onto the smallest thread of hope, so I'll follow your plan.
FRIAR FRANCIS 'Tis well consented: presently away; For to strange sores strangely they strain the cure. Come, lady, die to live: this wedding-day Perhaps is but prolong'd: have patience and endure.	**FRIAR FRANCIS** Well done for agreeing! For now, we'll go our separate ways; 'strange sores need strange cures' as they say. Come, lady Hero, die to live: hopefully this wedding-day is just postponed: have patience and endure.
Exeunt all but BENEDICK and BEATRICE	*Exeunt all but BENEDICK and BEATRICE*
BENEDICK Lady Beatrice, have you wept all this while?	**BENEDICK** Lady Beatrice, have you been crying all this time?
BEATRICE Yea, and I will weep a while longer.	**BEATRICE** Yes, and I will weep even more.
BENEDICK I will not desire that.	**BENEDICK** I don't want you to do that.
BEATRICE You have no reason; I do it freely.	**BEATRICE** I'm not doing it for you; I do it freely.
BENEDICK Surely I do believe your fair cousin is wronged.	**BENEDICK** I really do believe your lovely cousin Hero has been wronged.
BEATRICE Ah, how much might the man deserve of me that would right her!	**BEATRICE** Ah, how I'd reward the man who could avenge her!
BENEDICK Is there any way to show such friendship?	**BENEDICK** Is there any way to show such friendship?

BEATRICE A very even way, but no such friend.	**BEATRICE** Oh easily, but no such friend who'd do it.
BENEDICK May a man do it?	**BENEDICK** Could a man do it?
BEATRICE It is a man's office, but not yours.	**BEATRICE** It is a man's job, but not yours.
BENEDICK I do love nothing in the world so well as you: is not that strange?	**BENEDICK** I love you more than anything in the world: isn't that strange?
BEATRICE As strange as the thing I know not. It were as possible for me to say I loved nothing so well as you: but believe me not; and yet I lie not; I confess nothing, nor I deny nothing. I am sorry for my cousin.	**BEATRICE** As strange as – oh I don't know! I could say I love nothing as much as you: but don't believe me; even though I'm not lying; I'm not confessing anything, nor am I denying anything. I'm just sorry for my cousin.
BENEDICK By my sword, Beatrice, thou lovest me.	**BENEDICK** By my sword, Beatrice, I swear you love me.
BEATRICE Do not swear, and eat it.	**BEATRICE** Don't swear it, then eat your words later.
BENEDICK I will swear by it that you love me; and I will make him eat it that says I love not you.	**BENEDICK** I will swear that you love me; and I will make anyone who that says I don't love you eat his words.
BEATRICE Will you not eat your word?	**BEATRICE** You won't eat your words?
BENEDICK With no sauce that can be devised to it. I protest I love thee.	**BENEDICK** Not even with delicious sauce! I promise, it's true: I love you.
BEATRICE Why, then, God forgive me!	**BEATRICE** In that case, God forgive me!
BENEDICK What offence, sweet Beatrice?	**BENEDICK** What have you done, sweet Beatrice?
BEATRICE You have stayed me in a happy hour: I was about to protest I loved you.	**BEATRICE** You have stopped me at a good time: I was about to say I loved you.
BENEDICK And do it with all thy heart.	**BENEDICK** So do it with all your heart.
BEATRICE I love you with so much of my heart that none is left to protest.	**BEATRICE** I love you with so much of my heart that none is left to proclaim it.
BENEDICK Come, bid me do any thing for thee.	**BENEDICK** Come, ask me to do anything for you.

BEATRICE Kill Claudio.	**BEATRICE** Kill Claudio.
BENEDICK Ha! not for the wide world.	**BENEDICK** Ha! not for the wide world.
BEATRICE You kill me to deny it. Farewell.	**BEATRICE** You kill me by rejecting my request. Farewell.
BENEDICK Tarry, sweet Beatrice.	**BENEDICK** Stay, sweet Beatrice.
BEATRICE I am gone, though I am here: there is no love in you: nay, I pray you, let me go.	**BEATRICE** I am gone, even though I am here: there is no love in you: no, I tell you, let me go.
BENEDICK Beatrice,--	**BENEDICK** Beatrice,--
BEATRICE In faith, I will go.	**BEATRICE** In faith, I will go.
BENEDICK We'll be friends first.	**BENEDICK** We'll be friends first.
BEATRICE You dare easier be friends with me than fight with mine enemy.	**BEATRICE** You dare try to be friends with me when you won't fight with mine enemy?
BENEDICK Is Claudio thine enemy?	**BENEDICK** Is Claudio really your enemy?
BEATRICE Is he not approved in the height a villain, that hath slandered, scorned, dishonoured my kinswoman? O that I were a man! What, bear her in hand until they come to take hands; and then, with public accusation, uncovered slander, unmitigated rancour, --O God, that I were a man! I would eat his heart in the market-place.	**BEATRICE** Hasn't he proved he's a huge villain? He slandered, scorned, dishonoured my relative! Oh if only I were a man! How could he! pretend everything is fine until they come to join hands; and then, in public, add to the accusation, blatant slander, vent pure hatered, --Oh God, if only I were a man! I would tear out his heart and eat it in public.
BENEDICK Hear me, Beatrice,--	**BENEDICK** Hear me, Beatrice,--
BEATRICE Talk with a man out at a window! A proper saying!	**BEATRICE** Talk with a man out of a window! unlikely!
BENEDICK Nay, but, Beatrice,--	**BENEDICK** Now listen, Beatrice,--
BEATRICE Sweet Hero! She is wronged, she is slandered, she is undone.	**BEATRICE** Sweet Hero! She is wronged, she is slandered, she is ruined.
BENEDICK Beat--	**BENEDICK** Beat--

BEATRICE Princes and counties! Surely, a princely testimony, a goodly count, Count Comfect; a sweet gallant, surely! O that I were a man for his sake! or that I had any friend would be a man for my sake! But manhood is melted into courtesies, valour into compliment, and men are only turned into tongue, and trim ones too: he is now as valiant as Hercules, that only tells a lie and swears it. I cannot be a man with wishing, therefore I will die a woman with grieving.	**BEATRICE** *sarcastically* So much for Princes and counts! What a princely testimony, from a proper count, Count Sweetie-pie; a sweet gentleman, for sure! Oh if only I were a man I'd deal with him! or that I had a male friend to act on my behalf, but manliness has been melted into manners, courage into compliment. All this clever conversation turns men into tongues, and sleek ones at that: Claudio is now as heroic as Hercules who only tells a lie and swears it. I can't be a man by just wishing it, so I'll die a woman with grieving.
BENEDICK Tarry, good Beatrice. By this hand, I love thee.	**BENEDICK** Wait, good Beatrice. With this hand, I promise I love you.
BEATRICE Use it for my love some other way than swearing by it.	**BEATRICE** Use it for my love some other way than just swearing by it.
BENEDICK Think you in your soul the Count Claudio hath wronged Hero?	**BENEDICK** Do you really think you in your soul that the Count Claudio has wronged Hero?
BEATRICE Yea, as sure as I have a thought or a soul.	**BEATRICE** Yes, as definitely as I have a thought or a soul.
BENEDICK Enough, I am engaged; I will challenge him. I will kiss your hand, and so I leave you. By this hand, Claudio shall render me a dear account. As you hear of me, so think of me. Go, comfort your cousin: I must say she is dead: and so, farewell.	**BENEDICK** In that case, I'll do it! I will challenge him. I'll kiss your hand, and leave you. I promise, Claudio will be made to pay dearly. As you hear that I've kept my word, think of me. Go, comfort your cousin: I must say she is dead: and so, goodbye.
Exeunt	*Exeunt*

Analysis of Act 4 Scene 1

In this scene two key moments the audience has been waiting for happen: Claudio accuses Hero of unfaithfulness in public, bringing Don John's plans to fruition and, more subtly, Benedick confesses his love to Beatrice and she acknowledges that she loves him too, thereby fulfilling Don Pedro's plan.

Summary:
At he threatened to do at the end of Act 3 scene 2, Claudio accuses Hero of unfaithfulness publicly during the marriage ceremony. When he declares that he will not marry her because she is not a virgin, Leonato at first assumes that Claudio must have slept with her before the wedding, but then Don Pedro confirms that they saw Hero with a man at her bedroom window the previous night. Although Hero denies this, her obvious discomfort at what is being suggested – blushing- is taken as a sign of her guilt. When her father, Leonato, asks for a dagger to kill himself for shame, Hero faints. The accusers and guests leave, while Leonato gives way to self-pity, regretting that he ever had a daughter.

Benedick is the first to show any concern for Hero's wellbeing; he and the Friar believe that things are not as they seem and try to persuade Leonato to hatch a plan rather than disown Hero. Benedick, knowing Claudio and Don Pedro to be honourable men, suspects Don John has been up to mischief. The Friar, from observing Hero closely, is convinced that she is innocent. He suggests that as her accusers left when Hero swooned in a faint, they all pretend she actually died. This will have several good outcomes – firstly, Claudio will begin to feel sorry that she is dead and remember all the things he loved about her; having her 'dead' will also give them time to try and find out what the truth is and finally, if all else fails, she can quietly disappear into a nunnery, enabling the scandal to die.

Leonato accepts this plan half-heartedly, only because he doesn't know what else to do, but Benedick promises to play along, even though the accusers are his friends. This is a turning point in the play, because now he switches his allegiance from his comrades to Beatrice and her family. When the others leave and he and Beatrice are alone, Benedick offers to help put things right. When Beatrice refuses, he confesses his love to her. Her response is confused – she's not saying she does love him, but she's not saying she doesn't – in the end she says she's too upset to think about it. But for Benedick that is good enough. When he insists he wants to help, she orders him to kill Claudio. At first he refuses and she sees that as his being unfaithful to her, eating his words of love. When he is convinced by her argument that she would kill Claudio if she could, he agrees to challenge his friend to a duel to avenge Claudio's slander of Hero – and to prove his love for Beatrice.

Characters:
In this scene, Shakespeare contrasts the Elizabethan ideal of a nobleman and lover – Claudio- with the less attractive, down to earth Benedick. Instead of going to Hero to find out the truth, Claudio sets out deliberately to humiliate her, as he'd threatened to do when Don Pedro first planted the seed of doubt in his mind – this is not 'noble', it is 'natural'. Just as he did at the masked ball in Act 2 when he thought Don Pedro was cheating him by wooing Hero for himself, Claudio behaves petulantly rather than dealing with his anger – he says 'no' without explanation when asked if he's come to marry Hero, allowing Leonato to make a fool of himself by explaining it as a grammatical joke. At the point in the wedding ceremony where each has to declare that they know of no reason why they may not marry each other, Claudio elaborately builds up to his speech denouncing Hero as an 'approved wanton' or, as Don Pedro puts it, a 'common stale' – a prostitute. Although she clearly denies meeting a man, he takes everything she says as further proof of guilt.

Beatrice draws the audience's attention to this deliberate strategy when she explodes saying: *What, bear her in hand, until they come to take hands, and then* [in addition, doing it] *with public accusation, uncovered slander, unmitigated rancour?* In other words he has deliberately made as if nothing is wrong at first until the key moment of the wedding to make his rejection of her all the more dramatic – if he had ever loved her he would surely want to protect her from public humiliation. Later she calls him Count 'candy' because his gallantry (chivalry, thoughtfulness, courtesy) is sugary rather than real- she almost suggests that he would be enjoying the attention of being the wronged lover.

In contrast, Benedick – who in Act1 scene 1 made it clear he doesn't particularly like Hero- is concerned about her wellbeing: he's the only one to ask how she is! At the cost of his friendship with both Don Pedro and Claudio he is firstly prepared to help convince everyone that Hero is dead and later to challenge Claudio to a duel, either to kill Claudio or die himself. He is perceptive enough to realise – as no one else seems to – that Don John is probably at the root of the trouble. Loving Beatrice, he realises, is not about romance, but about being there for her when she most needs him. So he tries to find out why she feels Claudio has behaved dishonourably. While he's not afraid to say no to her, he listens to Beatrice's reasoning and is strong enough to change his mind.

Hero speaks 8 times, but only 127 words, 64 of those in one response to the Friar once out of the public eye. In contrast, Beatrice speaks 297 words in defence of Hero – that is not counting any talk about love for Benedick. This might suggest that Hero, representing the Elizabethan ideal, is unable to speak up for herself, unable to defend herself [yet capable, as shown in her response to the Friar], whereas Beatrice is not only *able* to speak, Benedick allows her to speak and hears what she says.

Context:
When Hero asks Claudio what the point of all his questioning ['catechising'] is, he answers strangely: *'To make you answer truly to your name'*, to which she replies, *'Is it not Hero? Who can blot that name with any just reproach? '* So it is clear that her name itself has special meaning. Shakespeare is alerting his audience to the significance of that name and most of them would have been aware of the Greek legend where Hero was the true love of Leander. He would swim across the Hellespont – a stretch of water 1km wide between the Aegean Sea and the Sea of Marmara- to meet her each night. When Leander drowned, she drowned herself as she did not want to live without him. To Shakespeare's audience, then, her name 'Hero' suggested faithfulness and loyalty.

Decoded in the light of this knowledge, in this odd exchange Claudio is asking her to prove her loyalty and Hero is saying *'how can you doubt it'*. When Claudio says: *'Hero itself can blot out Hero's virtue'* you have to wonder why he says 'itself' rather than 'herself'. It isn't a mistake. He is referring to the name 'Hero' spoken by Borachio. The audience knows it was actually spoken to Margaret [an example of dramatic irony], but poor Hero has no idea what he is talking about. Claudio is saying in subtext: *It is your name, Hero, spoken by the man at your window that has made me question whether you are as faithful as your legendary namesake, Hero.*

Language:
Shakespeare uses words like an artist uses colour or a musician uses combinations of notes.

- Repetition

We've just looked at how often the name 'Hero' is repeated in the space of 5 lines. In this scene it is used by Claudio 7 times in the first 93 lines, most often in connection with her character, rather than talking to her directly. Perhaps this is because he also calls her a lot of other things in this scene. He refers to her as the goddess Diana; the goddess Venus; a maid (i.e. virgin), or maiden many times; a 'rich and precious gift'; a 'rotten orange'; 'an approved wanton'; the Hero of legend; a 'hero'; 'most foul'; 'most fair'; 'pure impiety'; and 'impious purity'. In addition, Don John calls her 'pretty lady' and

Don Pedro calls her a 'common stale'. This is all within the first 100 lines of the scene. What should we make of that? Clearly Shakespeare is focusing our attention on Hero – we have to notice her in a way we haven't had to before. Perhaps we are also invited to wonder who, underneath all these different labels, the true Hero is. This 'ideal' Elizabethan woman seems in this scene reduced to a range of stereotypes.

Notice also how Leonato treats Hero: the first time he speaks directly to her in this scene is line 75, ordering her to tell the truth and then next only in line 116* to say 'Do not live, Hero'. In this speech he lurches randomly from speaking to her to speaking about her, and uses the word 'mine' seven times: for him the issue is his honour, not her pain or shame. After that speech, he only speaks about her, not to her, for the rest of the scene. His treatment of her brings home to us, perhaps even more than it would to Shakespeare's audience, who might regard his attitude as normal, that Hero is more of a possession to him than a person in her own right. Contrast his language with what the Friar says to her.

**Line 112 seems to be more an observation of her action that spoken to her.*

Structure:
This scene is made up of 2 focuses, Claudio's rejection of Hero and Benedick's declaration of love to Beatrice, with the plan to pretend Hero is dead as a bridge between the two, making 3 sections. The most important factor is that the structure highlights the contrasts: at first we examine the relationship between Hero and Claudio, then between Benedick and Beatrice. In between, Shakespeare contrasts Leonato and the Friar. One would expect the church to condemn Hero for her supposed sin of sexual immorality, whereas you'd think that Leonato, knowing his daughter, would find it hard to believe Claudio's accusation – surely he'd at least be asking her a few questions! Notice how it is the Friar who asks those questions, who believes her innocence and who ultimately devices a plan to save her honour, while Leonato is the one threatening to kill her and wishing she would die.

Themes:

- Love *vrs* status and honour

In this scene Shakespeare emphasises that when it comes to marriage, status and honour often mean more than love, even a father's love for his child. In Elizabethan times this was the case and may still be the case in some communities today. Notice all the 'dirty' imagery: 'rotten orange', 'common stale', 'pit of ink', 'stain' etc. – the 'love' in this 'marriage' seems squalid. In contrast, Benedick is prepared to sacrifice his status and honour as part of Don Pedro's elite set for the sake of his love for Beatrice, to fight for Hero's honour by challenging his friend Claudio to a duel.

Genre:
The trick of faking death was famously used by Shakespeare in his tragedy, *Romeo and Juliet*, written in about 1596, 3years before *Much Ado* (1599). Juliet drank a potion that made her seem dead, whereas Hero is just hiding; everything goes wrong with the friar's plan and Juliet eventually chooses to kill herself after Romeo has killed himself, whereas everything works out for Hero in the end, just as the friar planned it – and that's the difference between tragedy and comedy. Does it end in death or in potential new life?

ORIGINAL TEXT	MODERN TRANSLATION
A prison.	**A prison.**
Enter DOGBERRY, VERGES, and Sexton, in gowns; and the Watch, with CONRADE and BORACHIO	*DOGBERRY, VERGES, the Sexton (wearing his official gown) and the Watchmen enter, with CONRADE and BORACHIO*
DOGBERRY Is our whole dissembly appeared?	**DOGBERRY** Is our whole *dissembly* here?
VERGES O, a stool and a cushion for the sexton.	**VERGES** Oh - we need a stool and a cushion for the sexton. *A stool and cushion are brought. The Sexton sits.*
Sexton Which be the malefactors?	**Sexton** Who ones are the malefactors?
DOGBERRY Marry, that am I and my partner.	**DOGBERRY** That would be me, Sir, and my partner here.
VERGES Nay, that's certain; we have the exhibition to examine.	**VERGES** That's right; we have been *exhibitioned* to examine this case.
Sexton But which are the offenders that are to be examined? let them come before master constable.	**Sexton** What I mean is who are the offenders that are to be examined? Have them come up in front of the master constable.
DOGBERRY Yea, marry, let them come before me. What is your name, friend?	**DOGBERRY** Yea, indeed, let them come in front of me. *BORACHIO and CONRADE are brought forward* What is your, name, friend?
BORACHIO Borachio.	**BORACHIO** Borachio.
DOGBERRY Pray, write down, Borachio. Yours, sirrah?	**DOGBERRY** Please, write down "Borachio". And yours, lad?
CONRADE I am a gentleman, sir, and my name is Conrade.	**CONRADE** I am a gentleman, sir, and my name is Conrade.
DOGBERRY Write down, master gentleman Conrade. Masters, do you serve God?	**DOGBERRY** Write down, "Master Gentleman Conrade". Masters, do you serve God?
CONRADE BORACHIO Yea, sir, we hope.	**CONRADE and BORACHIO** Yes, sir, we hope so.

DOGBERRY Write down, that they hope they serve God: and write God first; for God defend but God should go before such villains! Masters, it is proved already that you are little better than false knaves; and it will go near to be thought so shortly. How answer you for yourselves?	**DOGBERRY** Write down, that they hope they serve God. But write "God" first - God forbid that such villains should be put before God! Masters, it has already been proved that you are little more than lying scoundrels, it will soon be common knowledge. What do you have to say for yourselves?
CONRADE Marry, sir, we say we are none.	**CONRADE** Truthfully, sir, we say we are not scoundrels.
DOGBERRY A marvellous witty fellow, I assure you: but I will go about with him. Come you hither, sirrah; a word in your ear: sir, I say to you, it is thought you are false knaves.	**DOGBERRY** A very cunning fellow, for sure, but I will get the better of him. Come to me, lad - let me give you a word in your ear: sir, I tell you, we believe you both to be lying scoundrels.
BORACHIO Sir, I say to you we are none.	**BORACHIO** And I tell to you we are not, Sir.
DOGBERRY Well, stand aside. 'Fore God, they are both in a tale. Have you writ down, that they are none?	**DOGBERRY** OK, that's all. I swear to God their stories match. Have you written that down, that they are not lying scoundrels?
Sexton Master constable, you go not the way to examine: you must call forth the watch that are their accusers.	**Sexton** Master constable, you're going about your examination all wrong: you must first call the men of the watch that accused them.
DOGBERRY Yea, marry, that's the eftest way. Let the watch come forth. Masters, I charge you, in the prince's name, accuse these men.	**DOGBERRY** Yes, for sure, that's the *eftest* way. Let the men of the watch come forward. Gentlemen, I command you in the Prince's name to accuse these men.
First Watchman This man said, sir, that Don John, the prince's brother, was a villain.	**First Watchman** This man said that Don John, the Prince's brother, was a villain, Sir.
DOGBERRY Write down Prince John a villain. Why, this is flat perjury, to call a prince's brother villain.	**DOGBERRY** Write down "Prince John a villain". Why, this is out and out *perjury*, to call a prince's brother a villain.
BORACHIO Master constable,--	**BORACHIO** Master constable,--
DOGBERRY Pray thee, fellow, peace: I do not like thy look, I promise thee.	**DOGBERRY** You be quiet, fellow: I don't like the look of you I'm telling you.
Sexton What heard you him say else?	**Sexton** What else did you hear him say?
Second Watchman Marry, that he had received a thousand ducats of Don John for accusing the Lady Hero wrongfully.	**Second Watchman** Why, that Don John had given him a thousand gold coins for wrongfully accusing the Lady Hero.

DOGBERRY Flat burglary as ever was committed.	**DOGBERRY** As clear a case of *burglary* as was ever committed.
VERGES Yea, by mass, that it is.	**VERGES** Yes, by what's holy, that it is.
Sexton What else, fellow?	**Sexton** What else, fellow?
First Watchman And that Count Claudio did mean, upon his words, to disgrace Hero before the whole assembly, and not marry her.	**First Watchman** And that Count Claudio intended, on hearing his words, to disgrace Hero in front of everybody who'd come for the wedding, and to not marry her.
DOGBERRY O villain! thou wilt be condemned into everlasting redemption for this.	**DOGBERRY** *(to BARACHIO)* Oh you villain! You will be condemned to everlasting *redemption* for this!
Sexton What else?	**Sexton** Is there anything else?
Watchman This is all.	**Watchman** That's all.
Sexton And this is more, masters, than you can deny. Prince John is this morning secretly stolen away; Hero was in this manner accused, in this very manner refused, and upon the grief of this suddenly died. Master constable, let these men be bound, and brought to Leonato's: I will go before and show him their examination.	**Sexton** And that is more than you can deny, gentlemen. Prince John secretly left town away this morning. Hero was accused and refused by Claudio exactly the way you described it - and died on the spot from grief. Master constable, tie these men up and take them to Leonato's house: I will go on ahead and show him the evidence.
Exit	*He exits*
DOGBERRY Come, let them be opinioned.	**DOGBERRY** Come, let's get them be *opinioned*.
VERGES Let them be in the hands--	**VERGES** Take hold of them --
CONRADE Off, coxcomb!	**CONRADE** Get your hands off me, fool!
DOGBERRY God's my life, where's the sexton? let him write down the prince's officer coxcomb. Come, bind them. Thou naughty varlet!	**DOGBERRY** As God's my life, where's the sexton? He should write down that the Prince's officer was called a fool. Come, on, tie them up! You wicked wretch!
CONRADE Away! you are an ass, you are an ass.	**CONRADE** Get off me, you ass! You are an ass!
DOGBERRY Dost thou not suspect my place? dost thou not suspect my years? O that he were here to write me	**DOGBERRY** Do you not *suspect* my position? Don't you *suspect* my age? The sexton should be here to write down

down an ass! But, masters, remember that I am an ass; though it be not written down, yet forget not that I am an ass. No, thou villain, thou art full of piety, as shall be proved upon thee by good witness. I am a wise fellow, and, which is more, an officer, and, which is more, a householder, and, which is more, as pretty a piece of flesh as any is in Messina, and one that knows the law, go to; and a rich fellow enough, go to; and a fellow that hath had losses, and one that hath two gowns and everything handsome about him. Bring him away. O that I had been writ down an ass! *Exeunt*	that I was called an ass! Remember I'm an ass, gentlemen, even if it was not written down - don't forget I'm an ass! You are full of *piety*, you scoundrel, as this witness has proved. I am a well-informed man and, what is more, an officer - and, what's more, a householder, and, what's more as good-looking a piece of flesh as anyone in Messina: and one that knows the law, so there!; and a rich enough fellow, so there!; and a man who's experienced a few losses in his time, but still has two robes and many fine things. Take him away! Oh if only the sexton had recorded that I'm an ass! *All exit*

Analysis of Act 4 Scene 2

After the drama of Claudio rejecting Hero during the wedding ceremony in the previous scene, the audience needs some comic relief, which is again provided by Dogberry and co.

Summary:
With a lot of fussing, the constables and the watch prepare to cross-examine Borachio and Conrade, while the sexton [usually the church official who rings the bells and digs the graves!] takes notes. It is the sexton who keeps things on track and gets the truth of what happened out of the night watchmen – as usual Dogberry is getting himself in a muddle by using the wrong words and getting sidetracked. Once he has heard the story, the sexton confirms that Hero was rejected at the altar on the false accusation Borachio staged, and consequently died, but also tells Borachio and Conrade that Don John has left them to take the rap by fleeing.

Genre:
Comedy aims to make the audience feel smugly superior by highlighting the silliness of the characters – think of the things people do in sitcoms that make us laugh. So Dogberry's incorrect use of language makes the audience feel good, as well as slowing down the action and easing the tension built up by the previous scene. These sub-plot characters are loved by audiences through the ages because they – Dogberry particularly – take themselves so seriously. Their misuse of language also makes them memorable.

Language:
The words Dogberry gets wrong have been italicised in the modern version: it is usually quite obvious what the word ought to be. Notice how Shakespeare makes Dogberry use a malapropism [misuse of words] in his very first sentence, when he calls an assembly a 'dissembly' – to dissemble means to mislead. The word 'eftest' seems to be one Dogberry [or Shakespeare actually] made up: perhaps is should be 'deftest' as in 'most deft' or best way.

Structure:
So far in this play, Shakespeare has always organised his scenes to contrast or echo each other, so thinking about why he puts these two scenes together might illuminate or reveal things we could miss on a superficial reading. There are some key similarities that draw our attention to the contrasts Shakespeare may want us to explore.

Although Dogberry seems a completely different character to Claudio, in Act 4 both suffer from wounded pride and make fools of themselves in their attempts to insist on their dignity. Claudio's behaviour is ignoble [dishonourable] in his desire to prevent being dishonoured, while Dogberry makes an ass of himself by insisting everyone remember he is an ass so that it can be noted.

Another similarity in both scenes is the way characters try to assess inner truths by outward signs – another aspect of the 'appearance vrs reality' theme. Hero's blushes are 'read' as shame rather than innocence, Dogberry lists all the outward signs – like two gowns- of his dignity, while displaying no dignity in his self-importance. These scenes explore similar issues in completely different ways.

Act 5 Scene 1

ORIGINAL TEXT	**MODERN TRANSLATION**
Before LEONATO'S house.	**Outside of LEONATO'S house.**
Enter LEONATO and ANTONIO	*LEONATO and ANTONIO enter*
ANTONIO If you go on thus, you will kill yourself: And 'tis not wisdom thus to second grief Against yourself.	**ANTONIO** If you go on like this, you'll kill yourself. There's no point beating yourself up about it.
LEONATO I pray thee, cease thy counsel, Which falls into mine ears as profitless As water in a sieve: give not me counsel; Nor let no comforter delight mine ear But such a one whose wrongs do suit with mine. Bring me a father that so loved his child, Whose joy of her is overwhelm'd like mine, And bid him speak of patience; Measure his woe the length and breadth of mine And let it answer every strain for strain, As thus for thus and such a grief for such, In every lineament, branch, shape, and form: If such a one will smile and stroke his beard, Bid sorrow wag, cry 'hem!' when he should groan, Patch grief with proverbs, make misfortune drunk With candle-wasters; bring him yet to me, And I of him will gather patience. But there is no such man: for, brother, men Can counsel and speak comfort to that grief Which they themselves not feel; but, tasting it, Their counsel turns to passion, which before Would give preceptial medicine to rage, Fetter strong madness in a silken thread, Charm ache with air and agony with words: No, no; 'tis all men's office to speak patience To those that wring under the load of sorrow, But no man's virtue nor sufficiency To be so moral when he shall endure The like himself. Therefore give me no counsel: My griefs cry louder than advertisement.	**LEONATO** For God's sake, stop telling me what I *should* do; Everything you say goes into one ear And out of the other. Stop giving me advice: I don't want anyone trying to calm me down Unless they've been through what I have. Find a father who loves his daughter like I do, Who is as proud of her as I am of mine, And let him tell me to be patient! Compare his misery with mine See if he can match me hurt for hurt, This to that, and one sorrow to another In each and every detail. If ***he*** smiles calmly and strokes his beard, Says 'not to worry', and hums instead of groaning, Takes comfort in wise sayings, and solves his grief With philosophy then by all means bring him to me And I'll follow his example! But trust me, he doesn't exist. People find it easy To offer advice in situations where They aren't suffering themselves: but when they are Their calm words turn into fury, and their own advice, Which they thought could cure the sickness of anger, Holds their rage back as weakly as a spider-web net, And they see that it's just hot air, unable to help. Everyone thinks that it's their job to tell Those who are suffering to be patient, But no one is able to be so calm And wise when they are suffering In the same way. So don't give me your advice: I'm too upset to pay it any attention.
ANTONIO Therein do men from children nothing differ.	**ANTONIO** Well then you're no different to a child.
LEONATO I pray thee, peace. I will be flesh and blood; For there was never yet philosopher That could endure the toothache patiently, However they have writ the style of gods And made a push at chance and sufferance.	**LEONATO** Please just be quiet. I'm allowed to be human: After all, there's never yet been a philosopher Who could endure the toothache patiently, No matter how wise And detached from pain and suffering.

<table>
<tr><td>ANTONIO
Yet bend not all the harm upon yourself;
Make those that do offend you suffer too.</td><td>ANTONIO
Yes, but what I'm saying is don't pile it all on yourself; Make the people who wronged you suffer as well!</td></tr>
<tr><td>LEONATO
There thou speak'st reason: nay, I will do so.
My soul doth tell me Hero is belied;
And that shall Claudio know; so shall the prince
And all of them that thus dishonour her.</td><td>LEONATO
Well, in that at least you make sense – I'll do it.
I know in my heart that Hero was falsely accused;
And I'll make sure Claudio knows, and the prince,
And everyone who dishonours her.</td></tr>
<tr><td>ANTONIO
Here comes the prince and Claudio hastily.</td><td>ANTONIO
The prince and Claudio are hurrying this way.</td></tr>
<tr><td>Enter DON PEDRO and CLAUDIO</td><td>DON PEDRO and CLAUDIO Enter</td></tr>
<tr><td>DON PEDRO
Good den, good den.</td><td>DON PEDRO
Good evening, good evening.</td></tr>
<tr><td>CLAUDIO
Good day to both of you.</td><td>CLAUDIO
Good day to both of you.</td></tr>
<tr><td>LEONATO
Hear you. my lords,--</td><td>LEONATO
Listen, my lords,--</td></tr>
<tr><td>DON PEDRO
We have some haste, Leonato.</td><td>DON PEDRO
We're in a hurry, Leonato.</td></tr>
<tr><td>LEONATO
Some haste, my lord! well, fare you well, my lord:
Are you so hasty now? well, all is one.</td><td>LEONATO
Oh, you're in a hurry my lord? Well okay, bye then!
In a hurry you say! Well it's all the same to me!</td></tr>
<tr><td>DON PEDRO
Nay, do not quarrel with us, good old man.</td><td>DON PEDRO
Come on now, don't fight with us old man.</td></tr>
<tr><td>ANTONIO
If he could right himself with quarreling,
Some of us would lie low.</td><td>ANTONIO
If he were still able to solve his problems by fighting some of us here would keep quieter.</td></tr>
<tr><td>CLAUDIO
Who wrongs him?</td><td>CLAUDIO
Who has wronged him?</td></tr>
<tr><td>LEONATO
Marry, thou dost wrong me; thou dissembler, thou:-
Nay, never lay thy hand upon thy sword;
I fear thee not.</td><td>LEONATO
You, you have wronged me you liar!
No, don't put you hand on your sword to scare me;
I'm not afraid of you.</td></tr>
<tr><td>CLAUDIO
Marry, beshrew my hand,
If it should give your age such cause of fear:
In faith, my hand meant nothing to my sword.</td><td>CLAUDIO
Oh dear me, curse my hand
For being so frightening to an old man:
I wasn't reaching for my sword, seriously.</td></tr>
<tr><td>LEONATO
Tush, tush, man; never fleer and jest at me:
I speak not like a dotard nor a fool,
As under privilege of age to brag</td><td>LEONATO
Damn you boy, don't smirk at me like that
I'm not talking like a foolish old man</td></tr>
</table>

What I have done being young, or what would do Were I not old. Know, Claudio, to thy head, Thou hast so wrong'd mine innocent child and me That I am forced to lay my reverence by And, with grey hairs and bruise of many days, Do challenge thee to trial of a man. I say thou hast belied mine innocent child; Thy slander hath gone through and through her heart, And she lies buried with her ancestors; O, in a tomb where never scandal slept, Save this of hers, framed by thy villany!	Who, because he is old, can brag about What he did while young, or what he would do If he was not so old. I'm telling you Claudio, That you have wronged my innocent child and me So badly that I must put aside my respectability And, with grey hairs and the other marks of old age, Challenge you to a duel. I say that you have slandered my innocent child; Your wicked lies have broken her heart, And now she lies buried with her ancestors In the family tomb; none of them were dishonoured Until she was disgraced, framed by your wickedness!
CLAUDIO My villany?	**CLAUDIO** My wickedness?
LEONATO Thine, Claudio; thine, I say.	**LEONATO** Yes, Claudio, yours!
DON PEDRO You say not right, old man.	**DON PEDRO** You're wrong, old man.
LEONATO My lord, my lord, I'll prove it on his body, if he dare, Despite his nice fence and his active practise, His May of youth and bloom of lustihood.	**LEONATO** My lord, I'll prove it by beating him, if he dares to fight, Despite his skill with swords and his constant training, His younger age and his manly strength.
CLAUDIO Away! I will not have to do with you.	**CLAUDIO** Get away from me! I'll have nothing to do with you.
LEONATO Canst thou so daff me? Thou hast kill'd my child: If thou kill'st me, boy, thou shalt kill a man.	**LEONATO** Do you think you can put me off so easily? You killed my child! If you can kill me, boy, at least you will have killed a man.
ANTONIO He shall kill two of us, and men indeed: But that's no matter; let him kill one first; Win me and wear me; let him answer me. Come, follow me, boy; come, sir boy, come, follow me: Sir boy, I'll whip you from your foining fence; Nay, as I am a gentleman, I will.	**ANTONIO** He'll have to kill both of us, and indeed we are both men: but that's not important - let him kill one first! So come on - beat me, and brag about it what do you say? Come, for me, boy - come on, Sir Boy, come, and get me! Sir boy, I'll make you fight, as sure as I'm a gentleman, I will!
LEONATO Brother,--	**LEONATO** Brother,--
ANTONIO Content yourself. God knows I loved my niece; And she is dead, slander'd to death by villains, That dare as well answer a man indeed As I dare take a serpent by the tongue: Boys, apes, braggarts, Jacks, milksops!	**ANTONIO** Don't you worry. God knows I loved my niece, and now she's dead - slandered to death by cowards who would no sooner dare to fight a real man than I would to grab a poisonous snake by its tongue! Boys, fools, braggers, louts, babies!

LEONATO Brother Antony,--	**LEONATO** Brother Antony,--
ANTONIO Hold you content. What, man! I know them, yea, And what they weigh, even to the utmost scruple,-- Scrambling, out-facing, fashion-monging boys, That lie and cog and flout, deprave and slander, Go anticly, show outward hideousness, And speak off half a dozen dangerous words, How they might hurt their enemies, if they durst; And this is all.	**ANTONIO** Relax! I know exactly what kind of men they are: petulant, impudent, fashion-crazy boys who lie and cheat and mock, defame and slander! They go around dressed like buffoons and acting tough, make a few threatening noises about how they will hurt their enemies, if they actually dared - and this is all.
LEONATO But, brother Antony,--	**LEONATO** But, brother Antony,--
ANTONIO Come, 'tis no matter: Do not you meddle; let me deal in this.	**ANTONIO** Come, it's no big deal: there's no need for you to be involved; let me deal with it.
DON PEDRO Gentlemen both, we will not wake your patience. My heart is sorry for your daughter's death: But, on my honour, she was charged with nothing But what was true and very full of proof.	**DON PEDRO** Gentlemen, we will not stay here to cause you more trouble. I am truly sorry for your daughter's death, but, I swear to you, we made no accusations for which we did not have proof.
LEONATO My lord, my lord,--	**LEONATO** My lord, my lord,--
DON PEDRO I will not hear you.	**DON PEDRO** I do not want to hear any more of this.
LEONATO No? Come, brother; away! I will be heard.	**LEONATO** No? Come then, brother, we let's go! I am determined that I will be listened to by somebody.
ANTONIO And shall, or some of us will smart for it.	**ANTONIO** You will be - or somebody here is going to suffer for it.
Exeunt LEONATO and ANTONIO	*LEONATO and ANTONIO both exit*
DON PEDRO See, see; here comes the man we went to seek.	**DON PEDRO** Look - here comes the man we were looking for.
Enter BENEDICK	*BENEDICK enters*
CLAUDIO Now, signior, what news?	**CLAUDIO** What news, Sir?
BENEDICK Good day, my lord.	**BENEDICK** Good day, my lord.
DON PEDRO Welcome, signior: you are almost come to part almost a fray.	**DON PEDRO** Welcome, Sir. If you'd come a minute earlier you might have been needed to stop what looked like developing into a fight.

CLAUDIO We had like to have had our two noses snapped off with two old men without teeth.	**CLAUDIO** We nearly both had our noses snapped off by two toothless old men.
DON PEDRO Leonato and his brother. What thinkest thou? Had we fought, I doubt we should have been too young for them.	**DON PEDRO** It was Leonato and his brother. What do you think? If we had fought, I fear the advantages of our youth would have been too much for them.
BENEDICK In a false quarrel there is no true valour. I came to seek you both.	**BENEDICK** If the argument is wrong, no amount of bravery can be right. I came to find you both.
CLAUDIO We have been up and down to seek thee; for we are high-proof melancholy and would fain have it beaten away. Wilt thou use thy wit?	**CLAUDIO** And we have been looking all over for you; we are feeling very sad and want to be cheered up. Will you use your wit to do it?
BENEDICK It is in my scabbard: shall I draw it?	**BENEDICK** My wit is in my sword-sheath: do you want me to draw it out?
DON PEDRO Dost thou wear thy wit by thy side?	**DON PEDRO** Do you then wear your wit by your side?
CLAUDIO Never any did so, though very many have been beside their wit. I will bid thee draw, as we do the minstrels; draw, to pleasure us.	**CLAUDIO** Nobody does that, though many people are beside their wits and don't think clearly. I call on you to draw your sword like I would call on musicians to play a tune, to give me pleasure.
DON PEDRO As I am an honest man, he looks pale. Art thou sick, or angry?	**DON PEDRO** I truly think he looks pale. Are you sick, Benedick, or angry perhaps?
CLAUDIO What, courage, man! What though care killed a cat, thou hast mettle enough in thee to kill care.	**CLAUDIO** Come on, Benedick! The proverb might say that 'worry killed a cat', but you've got enough courage in you to kill worries instead.
BENEDICK Sir, I shall meet your wit in the career, and you charge it against me. I pray you choose another subject.	**BENEDICK** Sir, I will meet your clever remarks with my own head on, like two knights charging at each other in a joust. Please keep your joking for somebody else.
CLAUDIO Nay, then, give him another staff: this last was broke cross.	**CLAUDIO** Give the man another lance - his last one broke because he got the attack wrong.
DON PEDRO By this light, he changes more and more: I think he be angry indeed.	**DON PEDRO** It seems to me that he is getting paler still: I think that he is indeed angry.
CLAUDIO If he be, he knows how to turn his girdle.	**CLAUDIO** If he is, then he should lighten up - it can't be anything worth fighting over.

<table>
<tr><td>BENEDICK
Shall I speak a word in your ear?</td><td>BENEDICK
Can I have a private word with you?</td></tr>
<tr><td>CLAUDIO
God bless me from a challenge!</td><td>CLAUDIO
God preserve me from a challenge to a duel!</td></tr>
<tr><td>BENEDICK [Aside to CLAUDIO]
You are a villain; I jest not:
I will make it good how you dare, with what you dare, and when you dare. Do me right, or I will protest your cowardice. You have killed a sweet lady, and her death shall fall heavy on you. Let me hear from you.</td><td>BENEDICK [Takes CLAUDIO aside]
You are a scoundrel. I'm not joking. I challenge you to a duel: you can chose whatever time and place and weapons you are brave enough for. Accept my challenge or I will tell everybody you are a coward. You have killed a sweet
lady, and her death and you will not get away with it lightly. Give me your answer.</td></tr>
<tr><td>CLAUDIO
Well, I will meet you, so I may have good cheer.</td><td>CLAUDIO
All right - I accept your challenge: it will be very entertaining.</td></tr>
<tr><td>DON PEDRO
What, a feast, a feast?</td><td>DON PEDRO
What, a feast? Are you talking about a feast?</td></tr>
<tr><td>CLAUDIO
I' faith, I thank him; he hath bid me to a calf's head and a capon; the which if I do not carve most curiously, say my knife's naught. Shall I not find a woodcock too?</td><td>CLAUDIO
Indeed he is; he has offered me 'a calf's head and a capon' - in the language of food, he's told me I should have allowed myself to be made a fool and a cuckold; If I don't use my knife very skilfully to cut off these insults, then it is worth nothing. Do you want me to add a stupid woodcock to the feast also?</td></tr>
<tr><td>BENEDICK
Sir, your wit ambles well; it goes easily.</td><td>BENEDICK
Sir, your wit saunters along at a very slow pace.</td></tr>
<tr><td>DON PEDRO
I'll tell thee how Beatrice praised thy wit the other day. I said, thou hadst a fine wit: 'True,' said she, 'a fine little one.' 'No,' said I, 'a great wit:' 'Right,' says she, 'a great gross one.' 'Nay,' said I, 'a good wit:' 'Just,' said she, 'it hurts nobody.' 'Nay,' said I, 'the gentleman is wise:' 'Certain,' said she, 'a wise gentleman.' 'Nay,' said I, 'he hath the tongues:' 'That I believe,' said she, 'for he swore a thing to me on Monday night, which he forswore on Tuesday morning; there's a double tongue; there's two tongues.' Thus did she, an hour together, transshape thy particular
virtues: yet at last she concluded with a sigh, thou wast the properest man in Italy.</td><td>DON PEDRO
I'll tell you how Beatrice praised your wit the other day, Benedick: I said that you had a fine wit - 'That's true,' she said, ' he has a fine little wit.' 'No,' I said, ' it is a great wit!' 'Alright,' she said, 'a great gross one.' 'No,' I said, ' it is a good wit.' 'That's true,' she said, 'it's quite harmless.' 'No,' I said, 'the gentleman
is learned:' 'O yes, he's such a learned gentleman,' she said 'No,' said I, 'he speaks many tongues [languages] ' ' Now that I do believe,' she said, 'for he made a promise to me on Monday night that he took back on Tuesday morning - that's two tongues at least that he speaks with'! She kept up this distortion of all your good qualities for a whole hour: in the end, though, she said with a sigh that you were the handsomest man in Italy.</td></tr>
<tr><td>CLAUDIO
For the which she wept heartily and said she cared not.</td><td>CLAUDIO
At which point she burst into tears and said she didn't care.</td></tr>
</table>

DON PEDRO Yea, that she did: but yet, for all that, an if she did not hate him deadly, she would love him dearly: the old man's daughter told us all.	**DON PEDRO** Yes, that's what she did - and yet if she did not hate you so much, she would love you dearly - that's what Hero told us.
CLAUDIO All, all; and, moreover, God saw him when he was hid in the garden.	**CLAUDIO** That's exactly it; and God saw him when he was hid in the garden, just like he saw Adam hiding in the garden of Eden.
DON PEDRO But when shall we set the savage bull's horns on the sensible Benedick's head?	**DON PEDRO** But when shall we put the "savage bull's horns" on the "sensible" Benedick's head?
CLAUDIO Yea, and text underneath, 'Here dwells Benedick the married man'?	**CLAUDIO** And written underneath: 'Here lives Benedick, the married man'?
BENEDICK Fare you well, boy: you know my mind. I will leave you now to your gossip-like humour: you break jests as braggarts do their blades, which God be thanked, hurt not. My lord, for your many courtesies I thank you: I must discontinue your company: your brother the bastard is fled from Messina: you have among you killed a sweet and innocent lady. For my Lord Lackbeard there, he and I shall meet: and, till then, peace be with him.	**BENEDICK** Farewell, boy: you know what I intend to do. I will leave you to gossip and banter away. Your mockery cuts no more than the sword of a boastful man who has broken his weapon to make out he has been in a battle. Don Pedro, my lord, I thank you for kindnesses, but I can no longer be your friend: your bastard brother Don John has fled from Messina, and between you you have killed a sweet and innocent lady. As for my Lord Babyface there, he and I shall meet in a duel. Until then, peace be with him.
Exit	*He exits*
DON PEDRO He is in earnest.	**DON PEDRO** He means it.
CLAUDIO In most profound earnest; and, I'll warrant you, for the love of Beatrice.	**CLAUDIO** Very much so: and, I bet you, because he's in love with Beatrice.
DON PEDRO And hath challenged thee.	**DON PEDRO** And he's challenged you to a duel.
CLAUDIO Most sincerely.	**CLAUDIO** And he meant that, too.
DON PEDRO What a pretty thing man is when he goes in his doublet and hose and leaves off his wit!	**DON PEDRO** What a pretty sight a man makes when he dresses up nicely to go out but leaves his wits at home!
CLAUDIO He is then a giant to an ape; but then is an ape a doctor to such a man.	**CLAUDIO** Such a man might look big to a fool, but in reality the fool is much cleverer than him.

DON PEDRO But, soft you, let me be: pluck up, my heart, and be sad. Did he not say, my brother was fled?	**DON PEDRO** Just shush for a minute and let me think: pull yourself together, my heart, and think seriously. Didn't he say that my brother has run away?
Enter DOGBERRY, VERGES, and the Watch, with CONRADE and BORACHIO	*DOGBERRY, VERGES, and the Watch enter with CONRADE and BORACHIO*
DOGBERRY Come you, sir: if justice cannot tame you, she shall ne'er weigh more reasons in her balance: nay, an you be a cursing hypocrite once, you must be looked to.	**DOGBERRY** Come on, Sir: if Justice can't make you give up your wild ways she might as well give up weighing right and wrong in her balance altogether. Anybody who swears and lies like you must be dealt with.
DON PEDRO How now? two of my brother's men bound! Borachio one!	**DON PEDRO** What's this? Two of my brother's men tied up! Borachio one them!
CLAUDIO Hearken after their offence, my lord.	**CLAUDIO** Let's hear what their offence is, my lord.
DON PEDRO Officers, what offence have these men done?	**DON PEDRO** Officers, what crime have these men committed?
DOGBERRY Marry, sir, they have committed false report; moreover, they have spoken untruths; secondarily, they are slanders; sixth and lastly, they have belied a lady; thirdly, they have verified unjust things; and, to conclude, they are lying knaves.	**DOGBERRY** Well, sir, they have lied; what's more, they have said things which aren't true; secondarily, they are slanderers; sixth and lastly, they have falsely accused a lady; thirdly, they have claimed that untrue things were true; and, to conclude, they are lying scoundrels.
DON PEDRO First, I ask thee what they have done; thirdly, I ask thee what's their offence; sixth and lastly, why they are committed; and, to conclude, what you lay to their charge.	**DON PEDRO** First, I ask you what they have done; thirdly, I ask you what their crime is; sixth and lastly, why they've been arrested; and, to conclude, what charge are you bringing against them.
CLAUDIO Rightly reasoned, and in his own division: and, by my troth, there's one meaning well suited.	**CLAUDIO** Well reasoned, and using his own logic too: and, truly, he's managed to dress up the same idea in many different ways.
DON PEDRO Who have you offended, masters, that you are thus bound to your answer? this learned constable is too cunning to be understood: what's your offence?	**DON PEDRO** What have you done to be tied up like this, gentlemen? this highly educated constable is much too clever for me to understand: what was your crime?
BORACHIO Sweet prince, let me go no farther to mine answer: do you hear me, and let this count kill me. I have deceived even your very eyes: what your wisdoms could not discover, these shallow fools have brought to light: who in the night overheard me confessing to this man how Don John your brother incensed me to slander the Lady Hero, how you were brought	**BORACHIO** Good prince, don't make me wait to tell my story in court: let me rather confess to you, and then let this count take my life. I have tricked your own eyes: these stupid fools have brought to light what you in your wisdom could not discover: they overheard me last night, confessing to Conrade

into the orchard and saw me court Margaret in Hero's garments, how you disgraced her, when you should marry her: my villany they have upon record; which I had rather seal with my death than repeat over to my shame. The lady is dead upon mine and my master's false accusation; and, briefly, I desire nothing but the reward of a villain.	here, how your brother Don John provoked me to slander the Lady Hero, how you were brought into the orchard and saw me court Margaret in Hero's clothes, and how you then disgraced her when you should have married her: they have a written record of my crime, for which I'd rather die now than have to repeat in court. The lady is dead because of my master's and my false accusation; and, in short, I want nothing other than the punishment I deserve for this crime.
DON PEDRO Runs not this speech like iron through your blood?	**DON PEDRO** His words stab me through the heart!
CLAUDIO I have drunk poison whiles he utter'd it.	**CLAUDIO** Hearing his words is like drinking poison.
DON PEDRO But did my brother set thee on to this?	**DON PEDRO** But did my brother really put you up to that?
BORACHIO Yea, and paid me richly for the practise of it.	**BORACHIO** Yes, and he paid me generously to do it.
DON PEDRO He is composed and framed of treachery: And fled he is upon this villany.	**DON PEDRO** Treachery is what he's made of, body and soul: And now he's run away from the consequences of his crime.
CLAUDIO Sweet Hero! now thy image doth appear In the rare semblance that I loved it first.	**CLAUDIO** Oh my darling Hero! now I remember your face once again as you looked when I first loved you.
DOGBERRY Come, bring away the plaintiffs: by this time our sexton hath reformed Signior Leonato of the matter: and, masters, do not forget to specify, when time and place shall serve, that I am an ass.	**DOGBERRY** Come, take away the *plaintiffs*: by now our sexton will have *reformed* Sir Leonato of the matter: and, gentlemen, don't forget to mention at the first opportunity, that I am an ass.
VERGES Here, here comes master Signior Leonato, and the Sexton too.	**VERGES** Here comes Sir Leonato with the Sexton.
Re-enter LEONATO and ANTONIO, with the Sexton	*Re-enter LEONATO and ANTONIO, with the Sexton*
LEONATO Which is the villain? let me see his eyes, That, when I note another man like him, I may avoid him: which of these is he?	**LEONATO** Who is this evil man? Let me see him, So that when I see others like him I'll know the signs to look out for: which of these men is the wrongdoer?
BORACHIO If you would know your wronger, look on me.	**BORACHIO** If you want to know who's to blame, I'm the one you should be looking at.
LEONATO Art thou the slave that with thy breath hast kill'd Mine innocent child?	**LEONATO** Are you the lowlife whose lies have killed My innocent daughter?

BORACHIO Yea, even I alone.	**BORACHIO** Yes, it's all my fault.
LEONATO No, not so, villain; thou beliest thyself: Here stand a pair of honourable men; A third is fled, that had a hand in it. I thank you, princes, for my daughter's death: Record it with your high and worthy deeds: 'Twas bravely done, if you bethink you of it.	**LEONATO** No, it isn't; you're being too harsh on yourself: Here are two honourable men, The third having run off, who are equally to blame. Thank you, princes, for my daughter's death: Be sure to add it to your long list of great deeds: It really was rather brave, when you think about it.
CLAUDIO I know not how to pray your patience; Yet I must speak. Choose your revenge yourself; Impose me to what penance your invention Can lay upon my sin: yet sinn'd I not But in mistaking.	**CLAUDIO** I don't know how I can ever ask for your forgiveness; But I have to try. Choose your revenge yourself; I will do absolutely anything you come up with To pay for my sin: but please believe me That I didn't do wrong on purpose.
DON PEDRO By my soul, nor I: And yet, to satisfy this good old man, I would bend under any heavy weight That he'll enjoin me to.	**DON PEDRO** Neither did I, I swear: But, if it would earn his forgiveness, I would also do any great task That this good old man asked me to
LEONATO I cannot bid you bid my daughter live; That were impossible: but, I pray you both, Possess the people in Messina here How innocent she died; and if your love Can labour ought in sad invention, Hang her an epitaph upon her tomb And sing it to her bones, sing it to-night: To-morrow morning come you to my house, And since you could not be my son-in-law, Be yet my nephew: my brother hath a daughter, Almost the copy of my child that's dead, And she alone is heir to both of us: Give her the right you should have given her cousin, And so dies my revenge.	**LEONATO** I cannot order you to make my daughter live; That would be impossible: but I beg you both To convince everyone in Messina That she was innocent when she died; and if your love Can create something from its sorrow, Write her an epitaph and hang it on her tomb. Sing the words to her bones; sing them tonight: Tomorrow morning come to my house, And since you could not be my son-in-law, Be my nephew: my brother has a daughter Who looks very like my own dead child, And she will inherit everything we own: Marry her, as you should have married her cousin: That is all I ask of you.
CLAUDIO O noble sir, Your over-kindness doth wring tears from me! I do embrace your offer; and dispose For henceforth of poor Claudio.	**CLAUDIO** Noble Leonato, Your kindness makes me want to cry. I gladly accept your offer; And put myself entirely in your hands from now on.
LEONATO To-morrow then I will expect your coming; To-night I take my leave. This naughty man Shall face to face be brought to Margaret, Who I believe was pack'd in all this wrong, Hired to it by your brother.	**LEONATO** I will expect your arrival tomorrow, then; For now I shall say goodnight. This vile man, Borachio, will be brought face to face with Margaret, whom I suspect was also hired by Don Jon to take part in this foul deception.

<table>
<tr><td>BORACHIO
No, by my soul, she was not,
Nor knew not what she did when she spoke to me,
But always hath been just and virtuous
In any thing that I do know by her.</td><td>BORACHIO
No, she wasn't, I swear!
She had no idea what was going on,
She has always been fair and honest
In everything that I have known her to do.</td></tr>
<tr><td>DOGBERRY
Moreover, sir, which indeed is not under white and black, this plaintiff here, the offender, did call me ass: I beseech you, let it be remembered in his punishment.
And also, the watch heard them talk of
one Deformed: they say be wears a key in his ear and a lock hanging by it, and borrows money in God's name, the which he hath used so long and never paid
that now men grow hard-hearted and will lend nothing for God's sake: pray you, examine him upon that point.</td><td>DOGBERRY
Even worse, sir, though admittedly not on record in black and white, this plaintiff here, the offender, called me an ass! I implore you, let it be remembered in his punishment.
And also, the watch heard them talk of someone called 'Deformed': they say he wears a key in his ear with a lock hanging from it, and borrows money in God's name, which he has done for so long without paying any back that now men grow hard-hearted and will lend nothing in God's name: please, question him about that as well.</td></tr>
<tr><td>LEONATO
I thank thee for thy care and honest pains.</td><td>LEONATO
Thank you for your efforts.</td></tr>
<tr><td>DOGBERRY
Your worship speaks like a most thankful and reverend youth; and I praise God for you.</td><td>DOGBERRY
You speak like a thankful and respected young man, your worship; and I praise God for you.</td></tr>
<tr><td>LEONATO
There's for thy pains.</td><td>LEONATO
Here, for your trouble. (Gives him money)</td></tr>
<tr><td>DOGBERRY
God save the foundation!</td><td>DOGBERRY
God bless you! May your house always stand.</td></tr>
<tr><td>LEONATO
Go, I discharge thee of thy prisoner, and I thank thee.</td><td>LEONATO
Go, I'll take charge of the prisoner. Thank you again.</td></tr>
<tr><td>DOGBERRY
I leave an arrant knave with your worship; which I beseech your worship to correct yourself, for the example of others. God keep your worship! I wish your worship well; God restore you to health! I humbly give you leave to depart; and if a merry meeting may be wished, God prohibit it! Come, neighbour.</td><td>DOGBERRY
It's a dangerous criminal I leave with you, your worship; I beg you to punish him personally, as an example to others. God bless your worship! I wish your worship well; God restore you to health! I humbly give you permission to leave; and if by happy chance we should meet again, God prevent it! Come, neighbour.</td></tr>
<tr><td>Exeunt DOGBERRY and VERGES</td><td>DOGBERRY and THE VERGES Exit</td></tr>
<tr><td>LEONATO
Until to-morrow morning, lords, farewell.</td><td>LEONATO
Until tomorrow morning, lords, goodnight.</td></tr>
<tr><td>ANTONIO
Farewell, my lords: we look for you to-morrow.</td><td>ANTONIO
Goodnight, my lords: we'll see you tomorrow.</td></tr>
<tr><td>DON PEDRO
We will not fail.</td><td>DON PEDRO
We'll be there.</td></tr>
</table>

CLAUDIO To-night I'll mourn with Hero. **LEONATO** *To the Watch* Bring you these fellows on. We'll talk with Margaret, How her acquaintance grew with this lewd fellow. *Exeunt, severally*	**CLAUDIO** Tonight I'll mourn Hero. **LEONATO** *To the Watch* Bring these men along. We'll talk with Margaret, and ask her how she came to know this degenerate man. *All Exit*

Analysis of Act 5 Scene 1

Again, this scene has two distinct parts to it and events already set in motion and expected by the audience are played out. At this stage of the play it is all about tying up the loose ends in preparation for the conclusion.

Summary:
The scene opens with Leonato expressing his grief and anger that Hero, whom he loved so much, has been so humiliated and lost her reputation – he just can't understand how it could have happened and won't be comforted by Antonio. His thoughts turn to revenge. At the same time, Don Pedro and Claudio come hurrying by and act as if they want to avoid the brothers, which makes Leonato even angrier. He and later Antonio seem to be picking a fight with Don Pedro and Claudio: it is clear to the audience that from both sides the happy relationship of Act 1 scene 1 has changed. Don Pedro defends Claudio's decision to make his accusations against Hero publicly and refuses to discuss the matter further. As Leonato and Antonio storm off, Benedick arrives. He issues his challenge, thanks Don Pedro for his kindness and resigns from his service. His parting piece of information is that Don John has fled.

It takes a few moments for the implications of this to sink in, but just as Don Pedro begins to wonder, Dogberry arrives with the prisoners. Where the first part of the scene was about issuing challenges, the second is about explaining the plot to disgrace Hero. Dogberry's story ends here with him still trying to get it on record that he is an ass.

Form:
This scene really relies on skilful acting, because it is very funny, but has to be played straight to have real impact. Both Antonio and Leonato seem to be psyching themselves up for a fight, but preventing each other from actually engaging. Given their ages, their posturing – huffing and puffing, rolling up their sleeves for a fight they couldn't hope to win – makes a staged version much more amusing than merely reading the words on the page. The important thing to bear in mind is that they know that Hero is not dead and so have to goad Claudio without actually doing any real damage to the relationship in the hope that things will go back to normal when the real explanation becomes clear.

When Benedick enters Don Pedro and Claudio are relieved – they've been looking for him and want someone to laugh with about Leonato and Antonios' threats- which only heightens the awkwardness when they discover he is not on their side. At first the friends try joking about in their old style using wordplay, but it soon becomes uncomfortably clear that Benedick means business – he hardly speaks, which is unusual for him – this is one of the ways in which Shakespeare emphasises his withdrawal from their friendship. [In the 64lines he spends on stage, Benedick speaks only 18, in 195 words]

The contrast between their exuberant horsing about and Benedick's seriousness is amusing, but the best productions make it uncomfortable: Shakespeare wants us to see through the 'sparkle' their status usually gives Don Pedro and Claudio to the silly, 'laddish' people they really are – they lose dignity in the eyes of the audience and it is Benedick we begin to respect and admire.

Even Dogberry should more tedious than amusing, so that the audience can share in the relief felt when Leonato finally gets rid of him.

Structure:
Like Act 4 scene 1, this scene has two focuses and three sections: 'challenges that bear witness to changed relationships', and 'realisations that lead to restoration as the true story is revealed' could be one way of describing the two issues it deals with. The three sections follow the characters: Leonato and Antonio blame Don Pedro and Claudio; Benedick issues his challenge and leaved Don Pedro's service; and Borachio explains what actually happened.

Characters:
Reading the opening 109 lines of the scene, you'll notice that all the characters have names ending in 'o'. Given how tightly structured the play is [e.g. repetition used in both structure and language to convey meaning – see previous analyses of scenes], we have to wonder whether that is just coincidence or whether it might link up again with the title, where 'nothing' could signify zero and represented by an 'o'. The 'body-language' of the play might be signalling that these once respected high-status characters have shown that they are not so great after all.

- Leonato and Antonio

The audience might have been able to believe Leonato's sorrow if it weren't for Act 4 scene 1, where it became clear that he only cares about *his* honour and reputation. His claim that he loved his daughter more than most men, sounds hollow after his order to Hero: 'Do not live'. In this scene both men are reduced to psyching each other up to pick a fight and hurl insults: they stand no real chance against two young soldiers. The supposed friendship between Leonato and Don Pedro is forgotten.

- Claudio and Don Pedro

This is another scene in which we see that wonder-boy Claudio is not the great man he seems. He is disrespectful to Leonato, mocking his age and even sarcastic: to Benedick he describes them – his hosts – as 'two old men without teeth'; whether literally true or not, he sees them as men without power and of an age where the teeth loosen in the gum. Don Pedro hides behind his position, refusing to discuss the matter with Leonato. Only when he hears of his brother's escape does he begin to feel uneasy about the conclusion they've drawn. All the strutting adds to their humiliation when they discover the truth.

Genre:
By making these high status characters behave in such an undignified way, Shakespeare is upsetting the natural order of society, which comedy does. Another difference between comedy and tragedy is that in tragedy there would be a price to pay for this lapse and the fall would be permanent, but being a comedy, they will be restored to their full status by the end of the play. However, Shakespeare always pushes convention a bit further and one could see that he has at least challenged the prevailing views [Elizabethan by intention, but also our own as we apply his story to modern society] of what is admired and what ought to be admired behaviour.

By implication marriage suggests children in the future and the continuation of the species, and this celebration of renewal is where the roots of comedy lie. So although to a modern audience it might seem ridiculous of Leonato to offer Claudio another girl to marry with an even bigger inheritance after he's shown his true colours, in terms of the conventions of comedy it is a desired or necessary outcome.

Act 5 Scene 2

ORIGINAL TEXT	MODERN TRANSLATION
LEONATO'S garden.	**LEONATO'S garden.**
Enter BENEDICK and MARGARET, meeting	*BENEDICK and MARGARET both enter and meet*
BENEDICK Pray thee, sweet Mistress Margaret, deserve well at my hands by helping me to the speech of Beatrice.	**BENEDICK** Please, sweet Mistress Margaret, do me a favour by bringing Beatrice to me so I can talk to her.
MARGARET Will you then write me a sonnet in praise of my beauty?	**MARGARET** Will you write me a sonnet in praise of my beauty in return?
BENEDICK In so high a style, Margaret, that no man living shall come over it; for, in most comely truth, thou deservest it.	**BENEDICK** Of such high quality, Margaret, that no living man will ever climb above it - you totally deserve that.
MARGARET To have no man come over me! why, shall I always keep below stairs?	**MARGARET** To have no man climb above me! Shall I always be the servant and never the mistress of my house?
BENEDICK Thy wit is as quick as the greyhound's mouth; it catches.	**BENEDICK** Your wit is as quick as the greyhound's jaws - it catches whatever it chases.
MARGARET And yours as blunt as the fencer's foils, which hit, but hurt not.	**MARGARET** And yours as blunt as a fencing foil: it hit's but does not hurt.
BENEDICK A most manly wit, Margaret; it will not hurt a woman: and so, I pray thee, call Beatrice: I give thee the bucklers.	**BENEDICK** Mine wit is most gentlemanly, Margaret: it will not hurt a woman - so, please, call Beatrice: I give in - I hand over my bucklers*.
MARGARET Give us the swords; we have bucklers of our own.	**MARGARET** It's the swords we want; we have bucklers of our own.
BENEDICK If you use them, Margaret, you must put in the pikes with a vice; and they are dangerous weapons for maids.	**BENEDICK** If you are going to use your bucklers, Margaret, you must screw the spike in - they are dangerous weapons for unmarried young ladies.
MARGARET Well, I will call Beatrice to you, who I think hath legs.	**MARGARET** Okay, I will call Beatrice - who doesn't need me to bring her - she has her own legs.
BENEDICK And therefore will come.	**BENEDICK** So she will come!
Exit MARGARET	*MARGARET exits*

Sings	**A buckler is a shield with a spike in the middle, used here for sexual innuendo* *Benedick sings to himself*
The god of love, That sits above, And knows me, and knows me, How pitiful I deserve,-- I mean in singing; but in loving, Leander the good swimmer, Troilus the first employer of panders, and a whole bookful of these quondam carpet-mangers, whose names yet run smoothly in the even road of a blank verse, why, they were never so truly turned over and over as my poor self in love. Marry, I cannot show it in rhyme; I have tried: I can find out no rhyme to 'lady' but 'baby,' an innocent rhyme; for 'scorn,' 'horn,' a hard rhyme; for, 'school,' 'fool,' a babbling rhyme; very ominous endings: no, I was not born under a rhyming planet, nor I cannot woo in festival terms.	The god of love, That sits above, And knows me, and knows me, How pitiful I am,-- I mean in my singing: but in loving, even the great lovers of Greek myths, like Leander and Troilus - and a whole book full of others with poetic names - were never driven so crazy with love as I am. But I just can't put onto verse: I have tried really hard, but I can't find any rhyme for 'lady' other than 'baby', which is silly, or 'horn' for' scorn' which wouldn't go down very well. For 'school' I can only think of 'fool', which is not much better than a baby's babbling; and 'baby' 'horn' and 'fool' are even worse when put together - they make me sound like a cuckold! : no, I wasn't born to be a poet, and I can't woo a lady with light-hearted pretty words.
Enter BEATRICE	*BEATRICE enters*
Sweet Beatrice, wouldst thou come when I called thee?	Beatrice, have you come because I called for you?
BEATRICE Yea, signior, and depart when you bid me.	**BEATRICE** Yes, sir, and I'll go when you tell me to.
BENEDICK O, stay but till then!	**BENEDICK** Oh, well please stay until then!
BEATRICE 'Then' is spoken; fare you well now: and yet, ere I go, let me go with that I came; which is, with knowing what hath passed between you and Claudio.	**BEATRICE** You've just said the word 'then', so I must say goodbye. But before I go, tell me what I came to find out: what passed between you and Claudio?
BENEDICK Only foul words; and thereupon I will kiss thee.	**BENEDICK** Nothing but unpleasant foul words: so now I can kiss you.
BEATRICE Foul words is but foul wind, and foul wind is but foul breath, and foul breath is noisome; therefore I will depart unkissed.	**BEATRICE** Foul words are just foul wind made of foul breath, and foul breath is nauseating - so I will leave without being kissed.
BENEDICK Thou hast frighted the word out of his right sense, so forcible is thy wit. But I must tell thee plainly, Claudio undergoes my challenge; and either I must shortly hear from him, or I will subscribe him a coward. And, I pray thee now, tell me for which of my bad parts didst thou first fall in love with me?	**BENEDICK** You've scared the word out of out of its real meaning with the force of your wit: But, in plain language, I have challenged Claudio to duel, and if he doesn't accept soon, I shall let it be known that he's a coward. So, now, tell me: which of my bad qualities first made you fall in love with me?

BEATRICE For them all together; which maintained so politic a state of evil that they will not admit any good part to intermingle with them. But for which of my good parts did you first suffer love for me?	**BEATRICE** For them all together - they all work so closely together that there's no room for any good in you at all. So you tell me - for which of my good parts first made you suffer love for me?
BENEDICK Suffer love! a good epithet! I do suffer love indeed, for I love thee against my will.	**BENEDICK** Suffer love! Well put! I certainly do suffer love, as I love you against my will!
BEATRICE In spite of your heart, I think; alas, poor heart! If you spite it for my sake, I will spite it for yours; for I will never love that which my friend hates.	**BEATRICE** In spite of your heart, rather, I think. Shame! Poor heart! But if you spite it for my sake, I will spite it for yours: I will never love anything that my friend hates.
BENEDICK Thou and I are too wise to woo peaceably.	**BENEDICK** Thou and I are too wise to woo each other peaceably.
BEATRICE It appears not in this confession: there's not one wise man among twenty that will praise himself.	**BEATRICE** You're arguing against yourself: very few truly wise men will praise themselves.
BENEDICK An old, an old instance, Beatrice, that lived in the lime of good neighbours. If a man do not erect in this age his own tomb ere he dies, he shall live no longer in monument than the bell rings and the widow weeps.	**BENEDICK** Maybe once, Beatrice, in a time where everybody knew each other. Now, if a man doesn't draw attention to himself, he'll be forgotten as soon as his funeral is over and the widow stops crying.
BEATRICE And how long is that, think you?	**BEATRICE** And how long will that take, do you think?
BENEDICK Question: why, an hour in clamour and a quarter in rheum: therefore is it most expedient for the wise, if Don Worm, his conscience, find no impediment to the contrary, to be the trumpet of his own virtues, as I am to myself. So much for praising myself, who, I myself will bear witness, is praiseworthy: and now tell me, how doth your cousin?	**BENEDICK** About an hour after the funeral and fifteen minutes after the crying stops. Therefore it makes most sense for clever people, conscience permitting, to blow their own trumpets as I do. But enough about me - though I do admit I am worthy of praise - how is your cousin, Hero?
BEATRICE Very ill.	**BEATRICE** She's not doing well at all
BENEDICK And how do you?	**BENEDICK** And what about you?
BEATRICE Very ill too.	**BEATRICE** I'm not doing at all well either.
BENEDICK	**BENEDICK**

Serve God, love me and mend. There will I leave you too, for here comes one in haste. *Enter URSULA* **URSULA** Madam, you must come to your uncle. Yonder's old coil at home: it is proved my Lady Hero hath been falsely accused, the prince and Claudio mightily abused; and Don John is the author of all, who is fled and gone. Will you come presently? **BEATRICE** Will you go hear this news, signior? **BENEDICK** I will live in thy heart, die in thy lap, and be buried in thy eyes; and moreover I will go with thee to thy uncle's. *Exeunt*	Serve God, love me, and you'll soon be better. But now I must end it there, as somebody is hurrying this way. *URSULA enters* **URSULA** Madam, you must come to your uncle's house. There's a right to-do going on. It has been proved that my Lady Hero was falsely accused, and the prince and Claudio were utterly deceived - and it was all Don John's doing, and he's run away ... come at once - please! **BEATRICE** Will you go with me to hear this news, sir? **BENEDICK** I will live in your heart, die in your lap, and be buried in your eyes - and what's more I will go with you to your uncle's! *All exit*

Analysis of Act 5 Scene 2

This is a 'meanwhile, elsewhere on the estate...' scene: it is happening more or less while the last bit of Act 5 scene 1's action is taking place. At the end of the scene Ursula brings news that Don John 'is the author of all', i.e. to blame. It also shows how relationships have changed through the action of the play, this time how Beatrice and Benedick express their love.

Summary:
Margaret, not yet knowing how she is implicated in Hero's downfall, cheerfully flirts with Benedick, who has asked her to fetch Beatrice for him – probably he wants to tell her he has recently challenged Claudio as promised. While he waits, Benedick tells the audience he can't write poetry and is no good at courtly love – as he puts it, 'I cannot love in festival terms'

He tells Beatrice about his challenge, and then they tease each other about being in love, each trying to be least affected. As Benedick becomes more serious and asks after Hero wellbeing, Ursula bursts in with the news that the plot has been uncovered and urges them to go up to the house with her to hear all about it.

Genre:
As with the previous scene, this scene involves the mocking of social conventions, in this case courtship or 'wooing'. In Elizabethan times love was often expressed in poems – the English/ Shakespearian sonnet originated then – riddles, coded messages etc. After a frustrated effort, Benedick rejects this method by saying, 'Thou and I are too wise to woo peaceably.' Shakespeare, a master sonneteer, makes Benedick really terrible at writing poetry for comedic effect – notice the sexual innuendo in 'scorn' and 'horn' being 'a hard rhyme', for example.

Context:
The ideal Elizabethan man – often referred to as Renaissance man – was both a soldier and a poet. People like, the great explorer and soldier Walter Raleigh, who also wrote many poems, typified the ideal. Being well educated in the Greek and Roman 'Classics', these men often alluded [referred] to characters in ancient literature, like Leander and Troilus, both famous lovers, often depicted in art. Songs, sonnets and blank verse were the traditional ways for a lover to express himself – women weren't expected to do the same, they were expected to receive attention graciously, but not let things go too far. Being slightly unattainable kept men making an effort. It is this sort of relationship Claudio and Hero represent, whereas Beatrice and Benedick have a more modern relationship, an equal partnership.

Act 5 Scene 3

ORIGINAL TEXT	MODERN TRANSLATION
A church.	**A church.**
DON PEDRO, CLAUDIO, and three or four with tapers	*DON PEDRO, CLAUDIO, and three or four others carrying tapers enter*
CLAUDIO Is this the monument of Leonato?	**CLAUDIO** Is this the Leonato's family tomb?
Lord It is, my lord.	**Lord** It is, my lord.
CLAUDIO [Reading out of a scroll] Done to death by slanderous tongues Was the Hero that here lies: Death, in guerdon of her wrongs, Gives her fame which never dies. So the life that died with shame Lives in death with glorious fame. Hang thou there upon the tomb, Praising her when I am dumb. Now, music, sound, and sing your solemn hymn.	**CLAUDIO** *[Reading from of a scroll]* Here lies Hero, Killed by slanderous words. Death, in repayment of these wrongs, Gives her fame which will never die - So though her life ended in shame Her glorious reputation will live on forever. *he hangs up the scroll* These words I hang from her tomb, Will go on singing her praises long after I am dead. Start the music, and sing the solemn hymn.
SONG.	*song*
Pardon, goddess of the night, Those that slew thy virgin knight; For the which, with songs of woe, Round about her tomb they go. Midnight, assist our moan; Help us to sigh and groan, Heavily, heavily: Graves, yawn and yield your dead, Till death be uttered, Heavily, heavily.	Please pardon, goddess of the night, Those that killed your virgin knight; For which offence, with songs of woe, Round about her tomb they go. Midnight, join us in sorrowful moaning; Help us in our sighs and groaning, Heavily, heavily: Graves, open wide and give up your dead, Until the last word about this death is said, Heavily, heavily.
CLAUDIO Now, unto thy bones good night! Yearly will I do this rite.	**CLAUDIO** Now, I will say good night to your bones, Hero! I will repeat this ceremony every year.
DON PEDRO Good morrow, masters; put your torches out: The wolves have prey'd; and look, the gentle day, Before the wheels of Phoebus, round about Dapples the drowsy east with spots of grey. Thanks to you all, and leave us: fare you well.	**DON PEDRO** Good morning, gentlemen; put your torches out. The wolves have had their fill for the night, and look, the soft colours of sunrise are appearing in the eastern sky. Thanks to you all, you can now take your leave - and fare well.

CLAUDIO Good morrow, masters: each his several way.	**CLAUDIO** Good morning, gentlemen. Let us each go our separate ways.
DON PEDRO Come, let us hence, and put on other weeds; And then to Leonato's we will go.	**DON PEDRO** Come, let's go and get changed - and then off to Leonato's.
CLAUDIO And Hymen now with luckier issue speed's Than this for whom we render'd up this woe.	**CLAUDIO** And may the god of marriage give us better luck than he gave Hero, who we've been mourning.
Exeunt	*All leave*

Analysis of Act 5 Scene 3

Some productions of the play leave this scene out as it seems rather dull and boring. Nonetheless, it does have symbolic significance as it represents a turning point: it is set at night and as Claudio leaves the tomb the sun is rising, representing a literal and figurative 'new day'.

Summary:
Claudio has promised (Act 4 scene 2) to write an epitaph to Hero and to sing to her bones before marrying Leonato's brother's daughter whom no one has seen: in this scene he fulfils the first stage of the promise to make up for 'killing' Hero. He has hired someone to read aloud a tribute to Hero at her tomb and someone to sing a song to her. In the song he promises to perform this ritual every year to commemorate her death.

Form:
Here there is scope for interpretation – some productions have Claudio reading and singing, some have him reading while someone else sings, some have him as a mere bystander. He ends by saying he hopes his next marriage will be more successful than his first. An actor could make the scene heart-rending as a contrite Claudio humbly expresses his remorse, or highlight how much of a business transaction marriage without real love can be by getting others to do it all on his behalf, going through the motions rather than really feeling wretched.

This whole scene is written in poetry, showing how solemn the occasion is.

Act 5 Scene 4

ORIGINAL TEXT	MODERN TRANSLATION
A room in LEONATO'S house.	**A room in LEONATO'S house**
Enter LEONATO, ANTONIO, BENEDICK, BEATRICE, MARGARET, URSULA, FRIAR FRANCIS, and HERO	*LEONATO, ANTONIO, BENEDICK, BEATRICE, MARGARET, URSULA, FRIAR FRANCIS, and HERO Enter*
FRIAR FRANCIS Did I not tell you she was innocent?	**FRIAR FRANCIS** Didn't I tell you she was innocent?
LEONATO So are the prince and Claudio, who accused her Upon the error that you heard debated: But Margaret was in some fault for this, Although against her will, as it appears In the true course of all the question.	**LEONATO** So are the prince and Claudio, who accused her because of the mistake you heard being discussed: But Margaret was partly to blame, Although against her will, it seems, Based on our investigation.
ANTONIO Well, I am glad that all things sort so well.	**ANTONIO** Well, I'm glad it all turned out so well.
BENEDICK And so am I, being else by faith enforced To call young Claudio to a reckoning for it.	**BENEDICK** So am I, otherwise my honour would force me to duel against young Claudio.
LEONATO Well, daughter, and you gentle-women all, Withdraw into a chamber by yourselves, And when I send for you, come hither mask'd.	**LEONATO** Now, daughter, and you ladies as well, Go into a room by yourselves, And come here wearing heavy veils when I call.
Exeunt Ladies	*Ladies Exit*
The prince and Claudio promised by this hour To visit me. You know your office, brother: You must be father to your brother's daughter And give her to young Claudio.	The prince and Claudio promised to arrive Around about now. You know your role, brother: You must pretend to be the father of your niece and give her to young Claudio.
ANTONIO Which I will do with confirm'd countenance.	**ANTONIO** My face won't give anything away as I do it.
BENEDICK Friar, I must entreat your pains, I think.	**BENEDICK** Friar, I must ask for your help, I think.
FRIAR FRANCIS To do what, signior?	**FRIAR FRANCIS** To do what, sir?
BENEDICK To bind me, or undo me; one of them. Signior Leonato, truth it is, good signior, Your niece regards me with an eye of favour.	**BENEDICK** To make me, or break me; one of them. Leonato; the truth is, good sir, That your niece sees something to love in me.
LEONATO That eye my daughter lent her: 'tis most true.	**LEONATO** She sees it with the eyes my daughter gave her.

BENEDICK And I do with an eye of love requite her.	**BENEDICK** And I feel the same way about her.
LEONATO The sight whereof I think you had from me, From Claudio and the prince: but what's your will?	**LEONATO** I think you see something in her because, Claudio, the prince and I opened your eyes to it: but what do you want?
BENEDICK Your answer, sir, is enigmatical: But, for my will, my will is your good will May stand with ours, this day to be conjoin'd In the state of honourable marriage: In which, good Friar, I shall desire your help.	**BENEDICK** I have no idea what you're talking about: But what I want is for you to give your blessing to what we want, which is to be joined today In the state of honourable marriage: That is why, good Friar, I'll need your help.
LEONATO My heart is with your liking.	**LEONATO** You have my blessing.
FRIAR FRANCIS And my help. Here comes the prince and Claudio.	**FRIAR FRANCIS** And my help. Here comes the prince and Claudio.
Enter DON PEDRO and CLAUDIO, and two or three others	*DON PEDRO and CLAUDIO, and two or three others Enter*
DON PEDRO Good morrow to this fair assembly.	**DON PEDRO** Good morning to you all.
LEONATO Good morrow, prince; good morrow, Claudio: We here attend you. Are you yet determined To-day to marry with my brother's daughter?	**LEONATO** Good morning, prince; good morning, Claudio: We've been waiting for you. Have you decided to marry my brother's daughter today?
CLAUDIO I'll hold my mind, were she an Ethiope.	**CLAUDIO** I'd go through with it even if she were an complete foreigner.
LEONATO Call her forth, brother; here's the friar ready.	**LEONATO** Call her here, brother; the friar's ready.
Exit ANTONIO	*ANTONIO Exits*
DON PEDRO Good morrow, Benedick. Why, what's the matter, That you have such a February face, So full of frost, of storm and cloudiness?	**DON PEDRO** Good morning, Benedick. Why, what's wrong? Your face looks like February, Full of frost, storms and cloudiness.
CLAUDIO I think he thinks upon the savage bull. Tush, fear not, man; we'll tip thy horns with gold And all Europa shall rejoice at thee, As once Europa did at lusty Jove, When he would play the noble beast in love.	**CLAUDIO** I think he sees himself as a wild bull, about to be tamed. Tut tut, don't worry Benedick: we'll make you look pretty and all of Europe will delight in you, just like Europa once delighted in Jove When *he* pretended to be a bull.
BENEDICK Bull Jove, sir, had an amiable low; And some such strange bull leap'd your father's cow,	**BENEDICK** When Jove was a bull, sir, his lowing sounded pleasant;

And got a calf in that same noble feat Much like to you, for you have just his bleat.	A similar bull mounted your father's cow, And in that same noble feat made a calf Very like you, for you bleat on in the same way.
CLAUDIO For this I owe you: here comes other reckonings.	**CLAUDIO** I'll get you for that: but there are other things to deal with first.
Re-enter ANTONIO, with the Ladies masked	*ANTONIO and the veiled Ladies re-enter*
Which is the lady I must seize upon?	Which is the lady I must marry?
ANTONIO This same is she, and I do give you her.	**ANTONIO** This is the one, and I give her to you.
CLAUDIO Why, then she's mine. Sweet, let me see your face.	**CLAUDIO** Why, then she's mine. Let me see your face my dear.
LEONATO No, that you shall not, till you take her hand Before this Friar and swear to marry her.	**LEONATO** No, not until you take her hand Before this Friar and swear to marry her.
CLAUDIO Give me your hand: before this holy Friar, I am your husband, if you like of me.	**CLAUDIO** Give me your hand: before this holy Friar, I am your husband, if you will have me.
HERO And when I lived, I was your other wife:	**HERO** And when I lived, I was your other wife:
Unmasking	*Lifting her veil*
And when you loved, you were my other husband.	And when you loved, you were my other husband.
CLAUDIO Another Hero!	**CLAUDIO** Another Hero!
HERO Nothing certainer: One Hero died defiled, but I do live, And surely as I live, I am a maid.	**HERO** Spot on! One Hero died in shame, but I'm alive, and surely as I live, I am a virgin.
DON PEDRO The former Hero! Hero that is dead!	**DON PEDRO** It's the former Hero! The Hero that died!
LEONATO She died, my lord, but whiles her slander lived.	**LEONATO** She was dead, my lord, only as long as the slander against her lived.
FRIAR FRANCIS All this amazement can I qualify: When after that the holy rites are ended, I'll tell you largely of fair Hero's death: Meantime let wonder seem familiar, And to the chapel let us presently.	**FRIAR FRANCIS** I can confirm that all these amazing things are true. After the marriage ceremony I'll go into more detail about Hero's 'death'. In the meantime, just accept that these wonderful things really happened, and let's get to the chapel right away.
BENEDICK Soft and fair, friar. Which is Beatrice?	**BENEDICK** One moment, friar. Which one of you is Beatrice?

BEATRICE [Unmasking] I answer to that name. What is your will?	**BEATRICE** [*Unmasking*] That's my name. What can I do for you?
BENEDICK Do not you love me?	**BENEDICK** Don't you love me?
BEATRICE Why, no; no more than reason.	**BEATRICE** No - not beyond what is reasonable.
BENEDICK Why, then your uncle and the prince and Claudio Have been deceived; they swore you did.	**BENEDICK** In that case your uncle and the prince and Claudio have been deceived: they swore you did.
BEATRICE Do not you love me?	**BEATRICE** Don't you love me?
BENEDICK Troth, no; no more than reason.	**BENEDICK** Truly no - not beyond what is reasonable.
BEATRICE Why, then my cousin Margaret and Ursula Are much deceived; for they did swear you did.	**BEATRICE** In that case my cousin Margaret and Ursula have been very much deceived, for they swore that you did.
BENEDICK They swore that you were almost sick for me.	**BENEDICK** They swore that you were almost sick with love for me.
BEATRICE They swore that you were well-nigh dead for me.	**BEATRICE** They swore that you were almost dead with love for me.
BENEDICK 'Tis no such matter. Then you do not love me?	**BENEDICK** Nowhere near! Then you don't love me?
BEATRICE No, truly, but in friendly recompense.	**BEATRICE** Absolutely not - except as a friend.
LEONATO Come, cousin, I am sure you love the gentleman.	**LEONATO** Come, come, niece - I am sure you love the gentleman.
CLAUDIO And I'll be sworn upon't that he loves her; For here's a paper written in his hand, A halting sonnet of his own pure brain, Fashion'd to Beatrice.	**CLAUDIO** And I'll swear to it that he loves her: In fact, I just happen to have here a slightly clumsy poem written to Beatrice in his own handwriting.
HERO And here's another Writ in my cousin's hand, stolen from her pocket, Containing her affection unto Benedick.	**HERO** And I have one in her handwriting which I stole from her own pocket, all about her love for Benedick.

BENEDICK A miracle! here's our own hands against our hearts. Come, I will have thee; but, by this light, I take thee for pity.	**BENEDICK** Well what a miracle! Our own hands are odds with our hearts! Come on then, I will marry you - but only out of pity.
BEATRICE I would not deny you; but, by this good day, I yield upon great persuasion; and partly to save your life, for I was told you were in a consumption.	**BEATRICE** I won't say no to you - as long as everyone realises that I'm only giving in to pressure - and also to save his life, as I was told he was wasting away with love for me...
BENEDICK Peace! I will stop your mouth. *Kissing her*	**BENEDICK** Oh be quiet! I will stop your mouth with a kiss. *Kissing her*
DON PEDRO How dost thou, Benedick, the married man?	**DON PEDRO** How does it feel to be Benedick the married man?
BENEDICK I'll tell thee what, prince; a college of wit-crackers cannot flout me out of my humour. Dost thou think I care for a satire or an epigram? No: if a man will be beaten with brains, a' shall wear nothing handsome about him. In brief, since I do purpose to marry, I will think nothing to any purpose that the world can say against it; and therefore never flout at me for what I have said against it; for man is a giddy thing, and this is my conclusion. For thy part, Claudio, I did think to have beaten thee, but in that thou art like to be my kinsman, live unbruised and love my cousin.	**BENEDICK** I'll tell you what, Prince: a whole college full of wise-crackers couldn't spoil my good mood. Do you think I care about being laughed at? If you're afraid of other people's witty comments, you won't dress up in your finery. In short - since I mean to marry, I will not listen to anybody who tells me not to - so don't try to throw my own words back in my face: people aren't always consistent, and that's an end to it. As for you, Claudio, I did think I might have to give you a beating, but since we are to be family, I'll leave you unbruised to love my cousin Hero.
CLAUDIO I had well hoped thou wouldst have denied Beatrice, that I might have cudgelled thee out of thy single life, to make thee a double-dealer; which, out of question, thou wilt be, if my cousin do not look exceedingly narrowly to thee.	**CLAUDIO** Well, I hoped you would refuse to marry Beatrice so I would have an excuse to batter you out of your single life and made you double-dealer - which I'm sure you'll turn into unless my cousin, your wife, keeps a sharp eye on you.
BENEDICK Come, come, we are friends: let's have a dance ere we are married, that we may lighten our own hearts and our wives' heels.	**BENEDICK** Come, come, we're all friends - let's have dance before we both get married to lighten the mood.
LEONATO We'll have dancing afterward.	**LEONATO** We'll dance after the wedding.
BENEDICK First, of my word; therefore play, music. Prince, thou art sad; get thee a wife, get thee a wife: there is no staff more reverend than one tipped with horn. *Enter a Messenger*	**BENEDICK** No - before! Come, musicians, play! Prince, you look sad: you should get a wife! A 'walking stick' tipped with horn is the most highly respected! *A Messenger enters*

Messenger My lord, your brother John is ta'en in flight, And brought with armed men back to Messina.	**Messenger** My lord, your brother John has been caught, and returned to Messina under armed escort.
BENEDICK Think not on him till to-morrow: I'll devise thee brave punishments for him. Strike up, pipers.	**BENEDICK** Forget about him until tomorrow - I'll come up with some splendid punishment for him. Play, pipers!
Dance	*There is a dance*
Exeunt	*All exit*

Analysis of Act 5 Scene 4

This is the grand finale, a double wedding – and right at the end, Don John gets caught, so that all the loose ends are tied up. Except that the marriages don't quite happen on stage as Benedick insists on a dance first...

Summary:
While they wait for Don Pedro and Claudio to arrive, the men chat about past events: the Friar being right about Hero's innocence, Margaret's part in the deceit and how Don Pedro and Claudio were tricked into mistaking Margaret for Hero. When the women are sent to prepare for the wedding and told to mask their faces in heavy veils, Benedick takes the opportunity to ask Leonato whether he may marry Beatrice and the Friar whether he will perform the service.

Leonato drops hints about how they tricked him into loving Beatrice and her into loving him – Benedick doesn't know what he is talking about, but the audience does. Benedick is very nervous – he has a 'February face' as Don Pedro puts it, so has to endure a lot of tiresome teasing.

Claudio discovers that his bride is actually Hero once he has sworn to marry her. All seems forgiven and the party prepare to move off into the chapel. Benedick asks for Beatrice and the couple have one last argument about whether they do love each other enough to get married – neither wants to submit first. When Claudio and Hero produce evidence in the form of the love poems, they give in and kiss. Don Pedro teases Benedick again, but he doesn't care and suggests the prince himself should marry. They prepare to dance before the actual marriage ceremony and just then news comes that Don John has been captured. Benedick urges Don Pedro to forget about it till the following day, when he himself will deal with the villain. So the dancing begins and the play ends.

Genre:
By the end of a comedy everything should be put right and the 'good guys' should be better off than they were before – this is the case here. Order has been restored, two couples married, the villains caught and unwitting transgressors like Margaret forgiven. 'Living happily ever after' is what an essential characteristic of comedy. There is some discussion amongst scholars as to why Benedick defers the actual ceremony, but Shakespeare probably didn't want to bother with the staging- it wouldn't add anything to have the wedding shown. Also, it would be more of an interruption to get the news of Don John's capture in the middle of the wedding, so probably it is more to do with practicality than a suggestion that Benedick is still unwilling to marry.

Language and structure:
The imagery introduced in Act 1 scene 1 of the 'savage bull' and Benedick looking 'pale with love' are referred to several times in this scene, giving the play a slightly cyclic structure, the effect of which is to enclose the drama. Claudio says of Benedick, '...he thinks upon the savage bull...we'll tip thy horns with gold' and Benedick himself suggests to Don Pedro that the most respectable walking stick for old age is one 'tipped with horn'.

Printed in Great Britain
by Amazon

35542379R00075